TO Mark

from
grandma
& Grandpa A.

Christmas 1997

Best Small Budget Self-Promotions

Carol Buchanan

NORTH LIGHT BOOKS
CINCINNATI, OHIO

Best Small Budget Self-Promotions Copyright © 1996 by Carol Buchanan.
Printed and bound in China. All rights reserved. No part of this book may be
reproduced in any form or by any electronic or mechanical means including
information storage and retrieval systems without permission in writing from
the publisher, except by a reviewer, who may quote brief passages in a review.
Published by North Light Books, an imprint of F&W Publications, Inc., 1507
Dana Avenue, Cincinnati, Ohio 45207. 1-800-289-0963. First edition.

Other fine North Light Books are available from your local bookstore, art supply store or direct from the publisher

00   99   98   97   96   5   4   3   2   1

Library of Congress Cataloging-in-Publication Data
Buchanan, Carol,
    Best small budget self-promotions / Carol Buchanan.
        p.   cm.
    Includes index.
    ISBN 0-89134-624-4 (alk. paper)
    1. Graphic arts--United States--Marketing.   2. Commercial art-
-United States--Marketing.   I Title.
NC1001.6.B83   1996
741.6' 068' 8--dc20   95-45514
                                                       CIP

Edited by Mary Cropper and Terri Boemker
Cover and interior designed by Angela Lennert Wilcox
Cover photography by Pam Monfort

The permissions on page 129 constitute an extension of this copyright page.

Dedication
To Buck,
the best salesman I ever met.

Acknowledgments
My thanks to the great designers
whose work appears on these pages.
They gladly took time to share their
expertise as well as their work, and
their generosity makes this book more
than a "pretty picture" book.

Thanks to Mary Cropper for thinking of me for this project, and for her
hard work and support along the
way. Also, thanks to Terri Boemker
for organizing the art and text, and
for bringing her own clarity and per-
spective to the project.

About the Author
Carol Buchanan runs her own graphic
design firm, C.A. Buchanan Design, in
Birmingham, Alabama; she has been
in business for herself since 1992. Her
firm offers graphic design and editori-
al services to the publishing industry.
Before starting her own company,
Buchanan was corporate art director
at F&W Publications, in Cincinnati,
Ohio for fourteen years. She is also
the author of *Quick Solutions for
Great Type Combinations* (North Light
Books).

Contents

4

Making
Special Occasions
Memorable

So many designers do holiday and special occasion-related self-promotions that you have to do something very special just to stand out from the crowd. And there's the problem of coming up with something that isn't overused, overworked or overdone. But it is possible. Discover how the designers whose work is showcased here have consistently come up with great promotions built around an intriguing theme or visual concept.

5

Benefiting by and
From Pro Bono

Ideally, a pro bono project gives you the chance to serve your community, or a cause you believe in, and to create a piece that will showcase your talents to potential clients. When it all goes right, everybody benefits. Here, you'll see how these designers were able to both contribute to the community and enjoy some creative freedom, including the opportunity to work in areas they wouldn't otherwise have had the chance to explore.

6

Collaborating for
Promotional Success

When it comes to creating and producing successful promotion pieces, collaboration can provide both cost and creativity benefits. All the participants benefitted from the collaborative projects featured here, and those successful relationships often carry over into other, client-driven projects. These designers share their insights into how to develop a project that will provide everyone involved with a great piece.

When we talk about "throwing money at a problem," we often mean that no one has taken the time to come up with a real solution — a greater investment of time and thought. We think we can make anything work if we just make it bigger, brighter, bolder or more colorful. But the best design solutions aren't always those with "more" because, over time, our audiences can adjust to the noise level of our communications and tune us out. When the audience in question consists of potential clients, that can be disastrous.

This book showcases the work of designers who have invested more time, thought and care than production dollars in their self-promotions. They've wrestled with questions about who they are, who they want to be and what they want to say. They've worked out concepts that help them communicate that message and then added appropriate visual elements, along with a lot of sweat equity, concern for quality and attention to detail.

The pieces you'll see here illustrate that the idea is more important than the execution. It's true: Good self-promotion doesn't require four-plus colors on press or any of the other visual fireworks that we love. Successful promotions come from designers who have the creativity to make excitement with one ink on press and from those with the savvy to squeeze four-color printing from a two-color budget. You'll find their stories and a lot of tips for your own promotion efforts in the pages that follow.

But before you start searching for inspiration, let's put the work you're about to see into context. What makes one self-promotion succeed where others fail?

In my fourteen years as an art director, I received a lot of self-promotion pieces. The best got thumbtacked to my wall. Now that I'm out on my own, my goal is to get my piece tacked to someone else's wall, or at least have it get an "honorable mention" when I see the client or follow up with a phone call. There are two things I've learned from being on both sides of the promotional equation. The first: Being remembered is the bottom line in self-promotion. If a prospect doesn't remember who you are or what you do, you won't get work. The second: You don't need to spend a lot of money to get attention. This is especially true when working with art directors, account executives, entrepreneurs and others in the idea business. Idea people appreciate good ideas that are thoughtfully (but not always expensively) executed.

The Idea Comes First

Executing a good design doesn't have to cost a lot of money. But first, make sure you have a good idea. How will you know when you have one? It will be appropriate for your audience — an issue of concern or a message the recipient relates to or finds thought-provoking or amusing.

Several studios, for example, reported a good response to promotions about the environment. Clearly, they tapped into an issue their audience felt strongly about. As another example, consider Mark Oldach's holiday promotions. These award-winning pieces are eagerly awaited by his clients. Why? Each is driven by a powerful concept with universal appeal, such as "the meaning of home and family" or "building a sense of community."

But a good idea doesn't have to be charming or lovable to provoke the right response. Graphik On!on has done several successful promotions inspired by a type of humor that many of their clients and fellow designers appreciated, although others thought it was rather twisted.

Once you've got your idea, plan your design and production as carefully as you would any other client's job. Sweating the details can pay large dividends; failure to pay attention to just one can ruin a great idea — or make it unaffordable. Consider some nontraditional methods of production to get a savings. For example, laser print your own labels, envelopes or even your business cards. Use an interesting rubber stamp or foil seal instead of embossing. Cut out a "die-cut" edge by hand.

Sandy Weinstein (Tin Box Studio) color-photocopied her moving announcements, but you can't tell just by looking at them. The full-color illustrations on the announcement combine original illustrations with stickers from a garage sale. Rodney Davidson (DogStar) created an award-winning self-promotion book that was originally put together with leftover scraps of paper. The hand-bound books are laser-printed as needed, usually on construction paper.

On the other hand, don't give up on an idea just because it's hard to fit into your budget. Consider bargaining with a client for samples or get permission to run onto a client's job. Or look for other creatives to share costs. When Tom Bonauro collaborates on a promotional piece with his long-time printer, he not only saves money but enjoys extensive creative freedom as well. Kenn Tompos helped a local photographer produce an eye-catching promotional poster that's attracted favorable notice from his own clients as well.

Vehicles for Self-Promotion

There are as many ways to promote your studio as there are designers. Most of us stick to the tried-and-true direct mail method, sending out targeted or shotgun mailings at least once a year. But there are other choices. Abney/Huninghake Design has found the "good, old-fashioned" press release to be an extremely inexpensive way to attract new clients. Studio MD uses an interactive portfolio disk. After the initial investment of time spent developing the program, ongoing costs involve only the price of a computer disk and reprinting a batch of the studio's specially designed computer disk labels. Jon Flaming developed some thank-you gifts for clients which were so well received that they have spun off into a separate business.

Although this is a book on self-promotion ideas that are inexpensive to produce, sometimes you can save money by investing in a small quantity of a single expensive piece. For example, even if you can't afford to print all of your promotion pieces in four or more colors, you may find it worthwhile to do a full-color capabilities brochure — just to show that you can. (Several designers I interviewed for this book stated that it's easier to get full-color work if you have a full-color promotion.) Mires Design, among others, subscribes to this philosophy; they have produced many wonderful one- and two-color promotional pieces, but they also have a beautifully printed full-color capabilities brochure.

Finally, keep in mind that promotions have increased impact when there is a strong visual thread — usually the studio's signature color or colors and typography.

Identity

To a certain extent, every contact you have with a client is an element of self-promotion. It helps if all the messages you send add up to a consistent overall picture of who you are and what you do. That's why it's so important that you have a clear vision of yourself and the kind of work you want to do before you start any promotional efforts. How often have you been furious with a client who didn't have a good handle on the objectives for a design job you were being handed? Then be a good client for yourself and think before you design. The best place to begin is with the first piece of self-promotion you'll probably do — your studio's identity.

It's wise to develop a mark that doesn't require full-color execution. Another money-saving move is efficient use of the whole printer's sheet, squeezing in labels and note cards you'll need. Consider running information that may become outdated far enough away from your logo that you can trim out cards or labels if your letterhead becomes obsolete. If you're sure you'll be moving, consider rubber stamping or hand-addressing a limited supply of letterhead for your current address. Or use rubber stamps to add seasonal messages to laser-printed letterhead.

Sharon Werner's striking stationery has a simple understated design that gets its impact from the powerful logo and interesting paper. Mark Evans' baseball-themed identity and promotional materials are effective in black only or when printed with some color.

Create an image for you and your studio. Be consistent in your choice of theme, logo treatment, color palette, etc. over several promotions to support an image of your work in the client's mind. Since your clients' jobs depend on their hiring the right people for projects, your promotions need to reinforce the decision that you're the right person. If you're doing a series of related pieces, plan ahead to keep costs down. What can you reuse from piece to piece? Can you pick up artwork or the paper from your identity system? Do you really need four-color printing or would fewer colors work as well?

Dia Calhoun, a lettering artist, has had great success with several series of promotional cards that show samples of her different script styles. The lettering samples change but the layout of the cards remains consistent, and the design of the promotion echoes the design and colors of her letterhead. This approach reinforces her identity while showing the many styles of lettering she can create. Phoenix Creative builds each year's unique holiday promotion around a central theme of the interpretation of being "hot." This approach showcases the studio's creative ability to bring something new to the same subject. It also fosters an association in the clients' minds that Phoenix is a "hot" creative shop.

Promote yourself with the kind of work you like to do. I've known illustrators who have received numerous assignments for a similar rendition of similar subject matter after they ran an ad in R.S.V.P. On the other hand, be sure to use a variety of pieces representative of the work you do. You don't want to become just "the guy who does fluffy dogs." Getting typecast can also be a problem if you do a loud, cartoony mailing that was appropriate for one occasion (Halloween, for example) that isn't typical of your usual work. Unless you are trying to break into a new industry or change the direction in your work, keep the piece you send faithful to the work you do.

Finally, you design for a living. So consider changing your identity, just to show what else you can do. A small design firm doesn't have the same agenda or audience that national brands have for their packaging. So be creative! Lanny Sommese doesn't feel constrained by his identity. He's redesigned several times. Barry Power and Rick Tharp routinely reinvent their identities, and in so doing, show their clients how they think — and have some fun while they're at it. Weigh the advantages of a design "facelift" over the benefits of repetition and recognition for your studio, and then decide for yourself.

Clients: Your Audience

Think of self-promotion as a vehicle for engaging in a dialogue with other designers as well as with your clients, since the two groups may overlap or be connected in other ways. Rick Tharp has received client referrals through his speaking engagements and promotions targeting other creatives. John Bielenberg's dialogue with top designers has enhanced his credibility both inside and outside of the design community and has led to client referrals as well as to a collaboration with other designers. Although targeted to local creatives, Winner Koenig's Russian deconstructivist-themed materials for the Tampa Bay Creative Club also attracted a favorable response from clients who saw them.

When you're first starting out, you accept any job that walks through the door. But, over time, the best designers find they are brave enough to let their clients know who they are, even if that means they aren't right for every project. While interviewing designers for this book, I heard over and over again about wanting clients who were a "good fit." That means clients who appreciate what you do and how you contribute to their business. Clients for whom you consistently do your best work and with whom you have a relationship built on trust. That's important, because the best — and cheapest — form of self-promotion is good word-of-mouth from satisfied clients.

Many people featured in this book use targeted mailing lists for their self-promotions. For example, to find and promote herself to the kind of art directors and agencies that she wants to work for, Lisa Adams combs through publications looking for people who are doing the kind of work that she would like to do. She then uses her carefully compiled mailing list for a series of self-promotion pieces carefully tailored to catch the eyes of this discriminating audience. John DeSantis has also had good luck with mailing lists; he drew on his background in publishing and marketing to plan his lists.

Choosing your audience is only a first step, however. Next you need to tailor your piece(s) to that audience. That doesn't mean you can't take risks with the right kind of client, however. Amy Quinlivan and Sharon Werner collaborated on a series of posters showcasing their talents for cutting edge design. The promotion might have been inappropriate for the local bank, but the hip clients they were seeking loved the series. They gained additional publicity when the posters were selected for inclusion in several important annuals.

Your mailing will often be more successful if it is targeted to the individual who receives it. This works especially well for mailings to existing clients, where you can personalize the promotion, and for carefully researched potential clients. For example, it's more effective to tell a publisher that you're a book designer and mention other publishing clients. Chris Conerley, a former ad agency art director, drew on his knowledge of agency life for a notepad promotion. He knew the pads would get used, keeping his name in front of potential clients.

In addition to improving your chances of getting the kind of work you want, targeted mailings limit the number of pieces you need to produce for each promotion. Nancy Doniger produces only a few of her exquisite mobiles each year because of the intensive handwork needed to create each one, but they are only sent to existing clients and excellent prospects. That also increases the value to the recipient — one reason Sayles Design gives out only thirty-six each of their special edition T-shirts. In many cases, having a limited quantity also means being able to spend more per piece without substantially increasing the budget for the entire project.

Keeping the Clients You Have

It's important to put as much or more energy into keeping your existing clients as into getting new ones. First of all, you've invested time in developing a good working relationship with your best clients. Established clients know and appreciate your work, so there is less opportunity for costly misunderstandings. If the client is small, you have an opportunity to make a huge impact on their success, as Vicki and Dick Rice of Artworks have discovered. Entrepreneurs trying to grow their companies welcome a designer who joins the team and furthers their goals.

Many of the designers featured in this book do regular promotions to keep current clients aware of what they've done lately. This is just good business; by keeping clients aware of the work you're doing, new directions, success stories, etc., you keep busy people reminded that you're available and doing exciting projects.

Some designers keep in touch with thank-you gifts, either at the holidays or whenever the spirit moves them, to continue building the kind of relationships that let them do good work. (For procrastinators, the holidays provide a deadline which must be met.) For example, Jon Flaming sends one-of-a-kind, handmade clocks and birdhouses to his clients, who express their appreciation both with words and more design work. The Design Company produces a limited number

of handmade or handcrafted packages each Christmas, and Vaughn Wedeen involves the whole studio in a brainstorming process for their seasonal promotions.

Pro Bono Pros and Cons

Sometimes the way to get noticed for your work is to donate your services. Many top designers built at least part of their reputation by doing just that. A lot of designers attract both local and national attention with projects for local arts organizations. Think how many people, both fellow designers and prospective clients, have seen Art Chantry's work on behalf of a wide variety of organizations.

The best pro bono work comes from the heart. Some designers are routinely asked to contribute their services, and have had to limit their causes to those they feel most strongly about. But a designer's contribution can make a big difference to nonprofit groups and those unable to pay a full fee. In turn, the designer receives the satisfaction of supporting a cause he feels deeply about, plus creative freedom and greater exposure. And, the causes you choose to support can send a message to those who see your credit line, attracting like-minded clients.

It's critical that you receive creative freedom in return for your services. (That doesn't mean six colors on press; it does mean support for your style and approach.) Your payment — a credit line and some samples — are meaningless if they don't position you where you want to be in the design or business community.

Some designers cite problems working with a board of directors for a nonprofit organization, and feel that they may have too many different people to please. (The designer's half of the bargain — creative freedom — is sometimes lost in the shuffle when this happens.) Others are more con-

cerned with the question of whether to purchase printing. Some designers contribute their expertise and contacts in purchasing the printing, and thus assure the quality of the final piece. Others choose not to make this commitment of time and resources. Still others worry about the implicit "debt" with a vendor who contributes to a cause. You'll have to pick your own way through the issue, guided by your relationship with vendors and the amount of control you need over the printing process. Art Chantry has built his reputation with a modest credit line on a large number of pro bono posters. He doesn't purchase the printing and welcomes the "surprises" that happen on press.

Creativity Breeds Success

We're in the business of communication. Attracting the right clients for your studio and keeping them doesn't have to mean spending a lot of money. In fact, I was very inspired in talking with the designers in this book (and even more inspired when seeing some of their pieces) with just how many different ways there are to be creative on a budget. But the key word here is "creative" rather than "budget." The thought and creativity come first — deciding on the message, selecting the best vehicle for communicating it, and determining the target audience. Then you figure out how to combine it all without spending a fortune. Whether you're trying to grow your business, or are happy with where you are and just want to maintain the client base you have, it's important to show existing and prospective clients the way you think, how you solve problems and the level of creativity you can bring to an assignment. The return on your investment will be a successful promotion for your most important client — you.

Developing the Studio's Identity

We sometimes forget about our identity system as a vehicle for self-promotion. In fact, it is your first communication with a prospective client, and provides your first opportunity to position yourself and stand out in the competitive design market. It's important to develop an identity that is faithful to your work and expresses your unique style and creative approach.

Every designer feels the need for a letterhead system, but there's no need to feel limited to the traditional elements of letterhead, envelope and business card (which isn't to say you can't do plenty with those basic pieces — you can, as evidenced in some of the pages that follow). The most successful systems reinforce the image you want clients to have of you and your work.

The studios in this section put a lot of creativity into developing and efficiently producing memorable and effective identities consistent with their design approaches. They've also looked for opportunities to get extra mileage out of their identities by application to a variety of promotional efforts.

Werner Design Werks Building an Identity Program

Now principal of Werner Design Werks, Inc., Sharon Werner was a senior designer at the Duffy Design Group, where she worked with such clients as USWest, Jim Beam, Fox River Paper Co. and Giorgio Armani. Since starting her own studio in December, 1991, Werner has developed a varied client list that includes Mystic Lake Casino, Fallon McElligot Advertising, Hunt Murray Advertising, Bloomingdales, Nickelodeon-MTV Network, Chandler Attwood (a division of Hon Industries), VH-1 Network, Musicland Stores Corp., Comedy Central and New York University. Werner has been recognized with awards and honors from Graphis, Communication Arts, *the American Center for Design, the New York Art Directors Club, the New York Type Directors Club, and British Design and Art Direction.*

Sharon Werner is the principal of Werner Design Werks, Inc. When she left the security of her position as a senior designer at the Duffy Design Group to open her own studio, she developed a plan for self-promotion that would take her well beyond the start-up stage.

She wanted even her initial promotional materials to be special without requiring a huge investment. She began building her identity with a striking, two-color logo that could be inexpensively run by a quick printer. Instead of having the logo applied to stationery, she had full sheets of the logo run and applied them to presentations.

Werner's next step was developing a self-promotion piece, "Samples," that would not only show off the studio's work but also be something that people would want to save. She decided to use a metal binder to make her presentation memorable and too attractive to be thrown away. The project would involve extensive handwork (which kept assembly costs down), but it would still be feasible if she targeted the promotion to a small number of people who were likely to be interested in her work rather than doing a huge, random mailing.

A full year after she opened her studio, Werner finally had her identity system printed in a trade with a printer. She carefully built on her already successful logo design, carrying her identity through cover sheets, envelopes in a variety of sizes, note cards, postcards, stickers and slide labels. She planned production so every square inch of each press sheet was used. Selecting the best size press sheets and planning the imposition

took more time, but the savings in paper alone were worth the investment.

Being in business for a year before printing an identity system has several advantages:

- You can better afford it.
- You have contacts with printers for possible trades.
- You can better determine the kinds and quantities of pieces you need.
- You know more about the kind of work you have and want, so you can better define and target your materials.

Although you're also less likely to be moving after a year in business, it's still wise to design with moving in mind. Werner took some subtle precautions in her note cards and postcards. The address is printed in black and often appears on the back, so reprinting will involve only a single plate change.

The final part of Werner's self-promotion is her pro bono work for the Children's Defense Fund (CDF), but her work for this special cause is more a labor of love than anything else. She got involved with the organization while working for Joe Duffy. Knowing her passion for this cause, he let her continue her work for the CDF after she left his studio.

Now that her self-promotion program has begun repaying her initial investment, Werner is seeking new ways to get her work noticed. Although the Samples promotion has been quite effective, she'd like to produce a new piece where she could do more than twenty-five books, perhaps something she could send in lieu of the "big portfolio."

Samples Book

Design: Sharon Werner

Metal manufacturing: Accuneering

Quantity: 25+ books

Budget: $5 to $8 per piece

The covers are the most expensive part of this eye-catching book. The samples of work inside are alternating pages of quick printed logo designs and color photocopies of other work. There's also a sheet giving Werner's qualifications. Since the books were assembled over time, some contain more samples than others, accounting for the $5 to $8 range in cost.

Beat the Odds
Invitation and Response Card
Client: The Children's Defense Fund
Account service: Susan Ellis, Fallon McElligot
Design: Sharon Werner
Illustration: Sharon Werner
Quantity: 4,000
Budget: Design donated

When work comes from the heart, it shows. Werner hustled to get all the services needed to produce this high-quality donated piece. Her goal for this pro bono work is not to win awards (although those have come, too), but to make a difference for a cause she cares passionately about.

**Werner Design
Werks Stationery**
Design: Sharon Werner
Illustration: Sharon Werner
Paper: Star White Vicksburg
Printer: Print Craft, Inc.
Embossing: McIntosh Embossing, Inc.
Quantity: From 2,000 to 8,000 pieces of each element
Budget: $3,000

Simpson Star White Vicksburg effectively showcases the design of Werner's identity. The design itself is strong but simple, gaining great impact from the unusual slate blue and "typewriter" type.

Werner prefers clasp envelopes to the kind that you have to glue to shut and cut to open. Although the custom envelope was more expensive than a printed stock envelope, she thinks that it was worth the investment. She had the envelope printed with another piece to save costs, and sent to a shop that does a large volume of envelope conversions. The high-volume shop gave her a better cost, but some envelopes were wrinkled. Werner uses the damaged envelopes to pay bills.

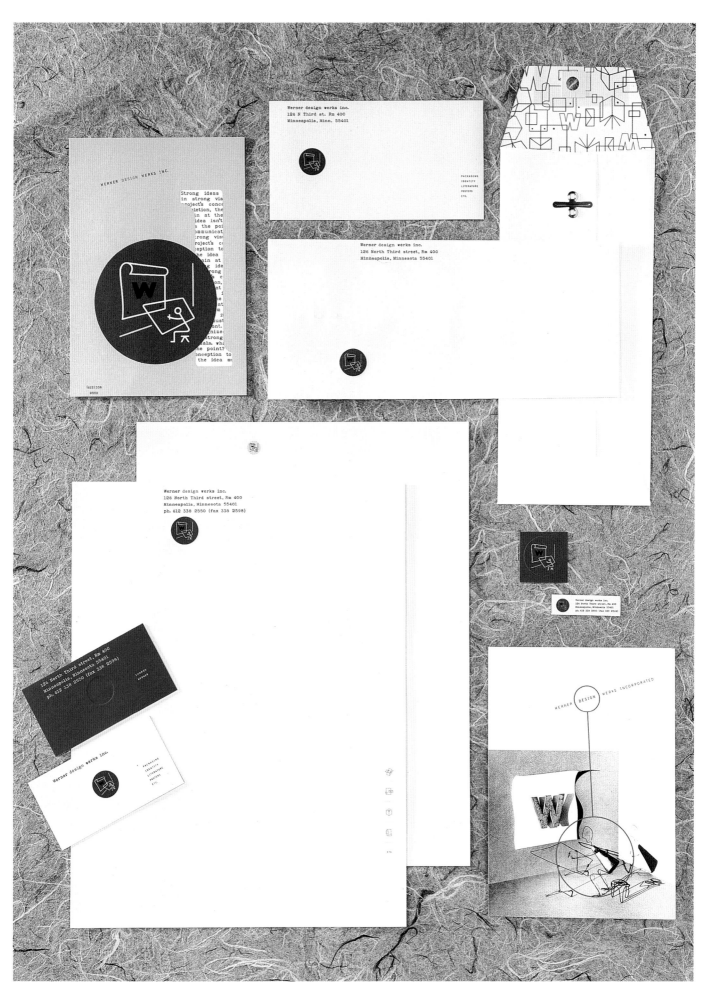

Designated Designer Designing a Distinctive Identity

Mark Evans, the designated hitter for Designated Designer, loves his work. He got his start designing wine labels for the wine his parents made at home, and majored in industrial design and visual communication at Ohio State University. Evans opened his design studio in Columbus, Ohio, in 1987; much of his work is logo design. He also operates a greeting card company and has marketed cards to several independent bookstores in Columbus. He has the name of the main character in his card line, Otto, on his license plate. The clients of his design studio include Nationwide Insurance, the Columbus Board of Education, Ameriflora, many local businesses and a variety of sports-related teams and events.

Mark Evans has created a distinctive identity for his Designated Designer studio. The name comes from the practice of having a designated replacement hitter (usually a power hitter) on American League baseball teams. He uses the baseball theme on his business cards and self-promotion brochure. Evans has also designed a baseball jersey that hangs in his studio and has a baseball hat in the works.

A baseball-inspired image may be a little unusual for a design studio, but Evans finds that his two baseball-themed promotional pieces — a self-mailing brochure and a business card that resembles a baseball card — are quite memorable and effective. He would like to do even more self-promotion, perhaps continuing his baseball theme.

The brochure serves as a mini-portfolio that quickly gives an idea of his design capabilities, including a wide range of clients and different styles. Evans wanted to show potential clients that he tries to find a unique solution for every logo design project he takes on. When he designs a logo, he knows it has to "work small," so he doesn't feel that showing a number of logos at a small size in the brochure compromises their quality. The business card with its baseball card-style graphics and humorous copy helps clients remember Evans when he calls to follow up on an initial contact or a potential project.

Evans feels that too many clients don't appreciate how important a logo can be to their business, so he works hard to educate them about how design can help them. Many of his logos have been done as a trade because that's how clients have wanted to work with him. For his part, these trades have given him the opportunity to indulge in a variety of sports-related activities. His interest in sports has also led him to do pro bono work for a number of sports-related events.

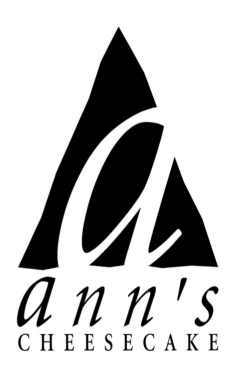

Logos
Art Direction: Mark Evans
Design: Mark Evans
Quantity: Varies
Budget: Varies
These are a few of the logos Evans designed pro bono or for trade with a variety of clients. Clockwise (starting at upper left): World Sun Bae Do Federation logo (traded for marital arts training), Ann's Cheesecake logo (traded for free desserts and discounts), the Capitol City Milers logo (traded for marathon training) and Cardia Heartfelt Greetings logo (done for a greeting card company the designer owns).

Designated Designer Brochure

Art Direction: Mark Evans

Design: Mark Evans

Quantity: 2,500

Budget: $1,425

Printed in black on 80-pound French Speckletone Chalk White cover stock, the printer ran a double black for coverage. The solid black adds a lot of drama to this one-color piece. The brochure has a friendly feeling that reinforces the baseball theme Evans chose for his studio's identity.

Baseball/Business Card

Art Direction: Mark Evans

Design: Mark Evans

Illustration: Mark Evans

Quantity: 2,000

Budget: $450

The business card was inspired by baseball cards that Evans collected as a boy. He includes his "statistics" and a short promotional blurb on the back, where baseball cards have statistics and "something fun" on them. He also gives a piece of Bazooka bubble gum with each card.

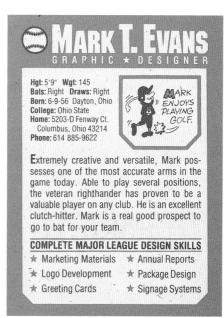

Matsumoto Incorporated From an International Perspective

In 1987, Takaaki Matsumoto cofounded M Plus M, Inc. In 1994, he became the sole principal and president; later that year the company changed its name to Matsumoto, Inc. Among the studio's clients in New York and Tokyo are The Equitable Gallery, Fashion Institute of Technology, The Gallery at Takashimaya, Maharan Fabric Corp., the Metropolitan Museum of Art, The Solomon R. Guggenheim Museum, Steuben, Sazaby, Inc. and Comme des Garcons. Matsumoto has been recognized with numerous honors, including awards from the American Institute of Graphic Arts (AIGA), the Type Directors Club, the STA 100 Show and the Art Directors Clubs of New York and Los Angeles. His work has been featured in various national and international publications, including Communication Arts, ID Magazine, Graphis, Metropolis, FP Design, Portfolio Design *and* International Contemporary Designers. *His work also appears in the book* The 20th Century Poster — Design of the Avant Garde.

Takaaki Matsumoto came to the United States from Japan in 1974, but he has kept a foot on both shores and maintained a global vision ever since. After attending the Art Center College of Design in Pasadena, he served as the art director for Knoll International in New York City. With a client base in both the U.S. and Japan, Matsumoto is committed to communication in the international design community. He currently serves on the board of directors of the International Design Network Foundation and the Worldesign Foundation, which work to put design organizations around the world in touch with each other.

In addition to supporting the international design community, Matsumoto, Inc. supports galleries in New York, notably the Equitable Gallery and Gallery 91. Matsumoto oversees the printing of invitations and posters for the galleries, but

keeps costs down for his gallery clients without compromising the design. Often done in one or two colors, the pieces rely on strong design and concept for visual impact.

Many of the self-promotion pieces that Matsumoto designed for M Plus M, which he founded with a partner, and for Matsumoto, Inc. are also striking examples of his concern for visual impact. He often uses the unique characteristics of unusual printing surfaces, such as Mylar, kraft paper or vellum, as part of his designs.

For its own communications, Matsumoto, Inc. has a large mailing list that was developed through research, referrals and a growing client base in the U.S. and Japan. Once or twice a year, the studio mails a promotional piece to the several thousand names on that list, including clients, prospects and vendors.

New Order Book
Design: Takaaki Matsumoto
Illustration: Takaaki Matsumoto
Quantity: 500
This book was an outgrowth of the "new order" poster ("91 Ways to Destroy the World") that Matsumoto was commissioned to create for Gallery 91. (The poster is shown on page 16.) Its message is the possibilities for a new world order following the fall of communism. The pieces were not mailed; they were given to clients and prospects.

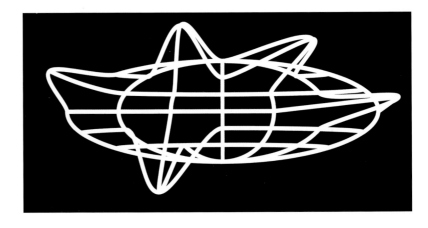

Strine Announcement

Design: Takaaki Matsumoto

Illustration: Takaaki Matsumoto

Quantity: 6,000

Strine Printing Co., a printer with whom Matsumoto had done work, approached him about doing the announcement for the opening of their New York City office. Matsumoto received a design credit for this six-color, die-cut piece.

The Music Box Project Invitation

Client: The Equitable Gallery

Design: Takaaki Matsumoto

Quantity: 3,500

Matsumoto designed this invitation for the opening of the Music Box Project at the Equitable Gallery in New York. Printed in black ink on UV Ultra, the invitation is translucent; interest is added with the graphic arrangement and layering of text.

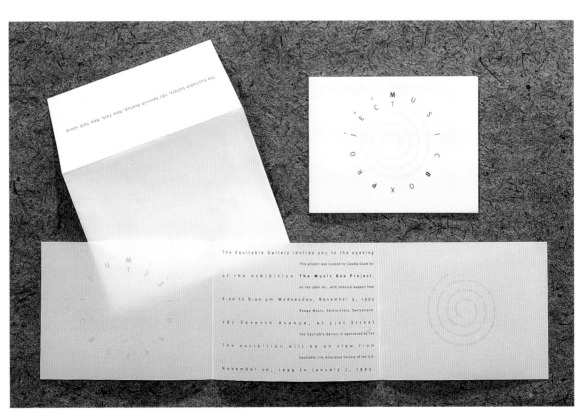

91 Ways to Destroy the World Poster

Design: Takaaki Matsumoto
Illustration: Takaaki Matsumoto
Quantity: 200

This poster, designed for Gallery 91, was the inspiration for the "New Order" book. The single color printing on each side (black on one side, yellow on the other) enhances both the powerful graphics and the stark typography. The strong message of the poster is better communicated through this simple treatment than it would have been with elaborate visuals or printing effects.

91 Ways to Destroy the World		
01 Racism	30 Fanaticism	61 Narcissism
02 AIDS	31 Fascism	62 Narrow mindedness
03 Abortion	32 Fashion victims	63 Nationalism
04 Animal testing	33 Film colorization	64 Noise pollution
05 Apartheid	34 Flattery	65 Nuclear disaster
06 Arson	35 Fraud	66 Nuclear weapons
07 Assault & Battery	36 Fundamentalism	67 Oil spills
08 Automatic weapons	37 Fur fashions	68 Plastic
09 Biological organisms	38 Gangs	69 Poaching
10 Blackmail	39 Genetic engineering	70 Politics
11 Brainwashing	40 Global warming	71 Pollution
12 Bribery	41 Greed	72 Racism
13 Burglary	42 Hate mongers	73 Rape
14 Capitalism	43 Homelessness	74 Religion
15 Censorship	44 Homophobia	75 Repression
16 Cheap champagne	45 Ignorance	76 Robbery
17 Cheating	46 Incest	77 Sexism
18 Chemical leaks	47 Infomercials	78 Shortsightedness
19 Child abuse	48 Insensitivity	79 Slavery
20 Conservatism	49 Insider trading	80 Solicitation
21 Corruption	50 Intolerance	81 Televangelists
22 Defamation	51 Junk bonds	82 Terrorism
23 Discrimination	52 Junk food	83 Torture
24 Dishonesty	53 Land fills	84 Toxic waste
25 Drug addiction	54 Larceny	85 TV dinners
26 Drug cartels	55 Loitering	86 Tyranny
27 Embezzlement	56 Loss of laughter	87 Vagrancy
28 Extortion	57 Money laundering	88 Vandalism
29 Famine	58 Monopolies	89 Vegetarians
	59 Mugging	90 War
	60 Murder	91 Xenophobia

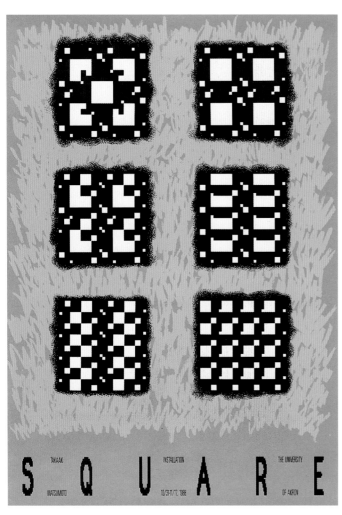

Square Poster

Design: Takaaki Matsumoto
Illustration: Takaaki Matsumoto
Quantity: 1,000

This poster was silkscreened on brown kraft wrapping paper for Matsumoto's show at the Akron Museum at the University of Akron. He was commissioned to create an original three-dimensional installation in a two thousand square foot space. The poster design represents the pattern of the installation.

M Plus M New Year's Card

Design: Takaaki Matsumoto
Quantity: 2,000

M Plus M's holiday card was a very graphic treatment of black type on reflective Mylar (offset printing). The second M in M + M is the reflection of the first.

Neo-Dada Poster and Invitation
Client: The Equitable Gallery
Design: Takaaki Matsumoto
Quantity: 3,500
The poster, printed in red and black on newsprint, and the invitation, printed in the same colors but on heavier stock, are reminiscent of the graphic woodblock Dada posters of the 1920s. The gallery papered its windows with three hundred of the posters. The invitations were folded in eighths and mailed to gallery patrons.

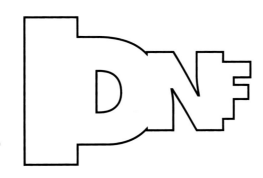

IDNF and Worldesign Logos
Design: Takaaki Matsumoto
Budget: Design donated
Evidence of his commitment to the international design community, these logos were done pro bono for both organizations.

Mires Design The Power of an Idea

Mires Design, established in 1983, is a twelve-person studio with a reputation for hard work, fresh ideas and good people. The San Diego firm has been recognized throughout the design industry by awards from Communication Arts, Print, *AIGA, the Society of Publication Designers and the New York Art Directors Club. Mires Design is proud of the longevity and quality of their client relationships. Deleo Clay Tile has been a client for ten years. The studio has done Ektelon's Total Racquetball catalog for five years and handled Adventure-16 store's twenty-four page, semi-annual newspaper since creating the chain's identity four years ago. Other clients include the American Cancer Society, DR Horton, Fieldstone Builders, Hewlett-Packard, Intel, LA Gear, Miller Brewing Co. and LaJolla Playhouse.*

Because Mires Design values their client relationships and hopes to maintain them, the studio puts an emphasis on staying in touch through promotions. The staff enjoys the opportunity to show the human face of the studio with actual photos of the staff and anecdotes about staff members in mailing pieces and announcements. The studio shares this philosophy with Bordeaux Printers, with whom they have collaborated on several promotions. These have been so successful for both businesses that they anticipate continuing to work together in the future.

Mires Design also takes the opportunity to address issues of importance to its principal and staff. A piece designed to promote the clients of artist's rep Celeste Cuomo had the theme of preserving and protecting the environment. Mires received overwhelming response to the piece, demonstrating how important this issue is to many people.

Many of the studio's promotions demonstrate the power of an idea. As the studio has demonstrated time and again, good design doesn't always have to have a big budget and six colors on press. Good design can be done with one- and two-color pieces that have a big impact. Some pieces amply illustrate the wisdom of getting more impact with a single splash of color than with colors spread throughout a piece. This is particularly effective on their logo mailers; the bright colors on the front panels capture the eye, while inside the logos stand out with only black ink on white paper. The contrast makes the piece even more memorable. Others demonstrate the power of black-and-white photographs as both great art and immediate, personal communication.

Sometimes an idea has to be shown in color. The joint promotions with Bordeaux Printers showcase everything from one- to four-color work. For Mires' own full-service brochure, on the other hand, the color is supplied only by the packaging for the aspirin tucked inside. The amount of color is also tailored to the audience. The studio's full-color capabilities brochure is their primary image piece. It shows a broad range of work and can be supplemented with printed samples or transparencies more specific to a client's needs. Although Mires Design needs to show its skill with limited color work in an age of ever tighter budgets, the studio doesn't want to be pegged as doing only that kind of work.

Mires Postcards

Art Direction: Scott Mires

Design: Scott Mires

Photography: Chris Wimpey

Quantity: 2,000 of each

Budget: Low

Mires Design developed this promotional series to remind clients who they are and to display staff personalities and creative thinking. A mutually beneficial trade was struck with the photographer. The concept of each card has been carefully carried through; a unified layout ties the diverse imagery and ideas together.

Promotional Mailers

Art Direction: Jose Serrano

Design: Jose Serrano

Copywriters: John Kuraoka, Kelly Smothermon

Quantity: 750 of each brochure

Budget: Low to moderate

Each mailer showcases Mires' expertise in a particular area. The simple, easy-to-produce design format ties the series together and permits quick distribution to current and prospective clients. Each brochure weighed no more than an ounce to keep postage down. The logo mailers show a sampling of the studio's unique and memorable logos. To economize, they limited selections to one-color plus black. The one- and two-color mailers were designed to show that well-designed one- and two-color pieces can make a big impact. Four-color printing was needed to showcase the successful packaging, so that piece was printed four over one.

Mires Moving Announcement

Art Direction: Jose Serrano, Scott Mires
Design: Jose Serrano
Photography: Chris Wimpey
Quantity: 1,000
Budget: Low

Sent to current and prospective clients, this piece provided a casual, fun way to introduce the staff while announcing the move. The photography was done as a trade for helping with the photographer's promotional materials.

Harcourt Brace Jovanovich Wrapping Paper

Art Direction: Scott Mires
Design: Scott Mires
Quantity: 500
Budget: Low

After a long year of work on a series of textbooks, Mires Design wanted to thank all of the people involved by giving them custom T-shirts that said, "I survived HBJ's Treasury of Literature." They used the work of many illustrators and incorporated the editors' comments about the illustrations in the design of the wrapping paper. The T-shirts and paper were a big hit. The studio was able to promote itself and thank everybody at the same time.

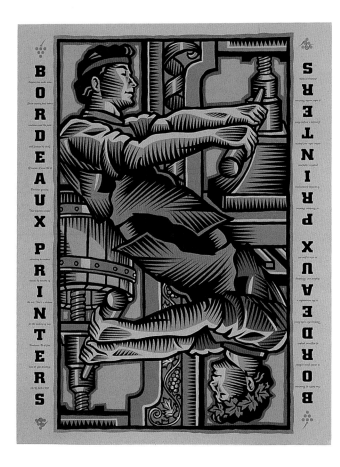

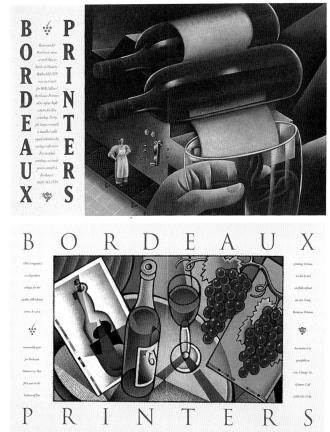

Bordeaux Printers Promotional Posters

Art Direction: Jose Serrano
Design: Jose Serrano
Illustration: Various illustrators
Quantity: 1,000 each
Budget: Costs shared with printer

Bordeaux Printers is a company that shares Mires Design's commitment to promotion on a regular basis. These three posters are typical of the series theme, which plays on the name "Bordeaux" to draw connections between printing and the art of making and appreciating fine wine. The collaboration on this series of posters proved quite successful for both organizations.

Bordeaux Printers Playing Cards

Art Direction: Jose Serrano
Design: Jose Serrano
Illustration: Tracy Sabin
Quantity: 3,000
Budget: Costs shared with printer

Bordeaux Printers wanted a playful promotional series that could be functional as well as nicely designed. The printer gave the cards to clients. Mires Design sent them as design samples to prospects.

Blink Identity Encore for Self-Promotion

Scott Idleman received a BFA in Graphic Design from the Kansas City Art Institute. He began his career in New York City, as the associate art director of the ill-fated Egg *magazine. He then worked for Double Space studio for three years. Idleman moved to San Francisco in 1992. He started Blink with fellow artist Nikki Ovitt, who then left to return to Albuquerque. Blink's clients include Levi Strauss & Co., Warner Bros., Giant Records and HarperCollins.*

The name of Scott Idleman's studio, Blink, comes from the TV show "I Dream of Jeannie." He describes the identity as "Middle Eastern filtered through Las Vegas; a kind of kitsch version of the Middle East." The distinctive logo, a combination of Middle Eastern style lettering and a stylized eye, inspired the background and cover of the self-promotion piece shown here.

Idleman is well aware of the importance of self-promotion and does a promotional piece every year. With this piece, he wanted to do something more elaborate, a piece that would also serve as a mini-portfolio. Idleman had gotten a lot of work from his full-size portfolio—his first, and still his biggest client, Levi Strauss & Co.— hired him on the basis of his New York portfolio, which contained lots of print material. However, he no longer wanted to send his whole portfolio out every time he contacted a prospective client. His final goal for the piece was to overcome the perception that he only works in a set style.

This brochure shows a lot of styles, yet all the pieces are tied together by the background and the game board style numbers and paths connecting them. The cover photograph and the inside envelope carry the Blink identity a visual step further. (The eyes on the ostrich feathers even contain the Blink logo.)

Blink Mini-Portfolio
Design: Scott Idleman
Photography: Rico Schwartzberg
Quantity: 2,000
Budget: $1,300

The brochure was run for free with another job. Idleman paid only for the business cards and envelopes. He waited for six months for the opportunity to run his brochure for free with a client's job. He had the piece ready to print when his chance came.

Tom Varisco A Signature Self-Promotion

Tom Varisco started his design studio in New Orleans in 1971. He has long been an active figure in the local design community and past president of the New Orleans Art Directors and Designers Association. Varisco also serves on the faculty of the Visual Arts Department at Loyola University. He has been profiled in Japan's IDEA *Magazine, Photo District News,* New Orleans *City-Business, HOW and* Communication Arts. *Clients include some of New Orleans's largest corporations, numerous medium-sized businesses and major nonprofit organizations, including Land's End, Willis & Geiger, New Orleans Jazz & Heritage Festival and the Aquarium of the Americas.*

Although Tom Varisco relies on networking and word-of-mouth in New Orleans for business contacts, he still occasionally gets requests for his signature self-promotion, the "Varisco/Nabisco" poster. This poster was inspired by an actual dialogue between Varisco and the national snack manufacturer. Varisco had designed cards and letterhead using a logo that resembled the famous Nabisco triangle. (He simply wanted to help people remember his name through a parody on the logo, creating an association with the rhyming names of Varisco and Nabisco.) Nabisco very nicely asked Varisco to stop using the letterhead and business cards, stating that the Nabisco triangle was a copyrighted symbol belonging exclusively to Nabisco. The corporation's lawyers and the designer's lawyers corresponded on the issue. Varisco "couldn't believe they would care" about his parody, but he finally agreed in writing to stop using the logo. On the way home from his lawyer's office, Varisco decided to do a poster based on his experience. The poster, appearing in several annuals, attracted more attention from fellow designers and potential clients than the identity system had, but didn't draw the wrath of Varisco's former adversary.

Varisco/Nabisco Poster

Design: Tom Varisco
Copywriter: Anna Zimmerman
Quantity: 1,000
Budget: $0 (Trade-out)
This poster was inspired by an actual dialogue between Varisco and the national snack manufacturer. Nabisco disapproved of Varisco using a logo on his cards and letterheads that was very similar to their famous red triangle. Varisco agreed to change his letterhead; this poster (which Nabisco did not find objectionable) drew more attention than the original identity system had.

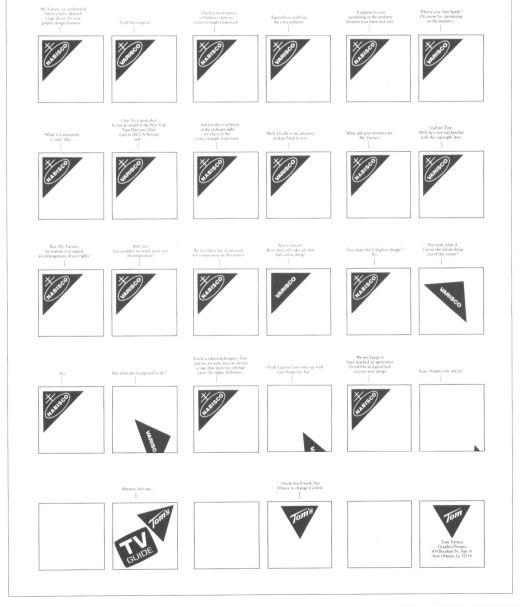

Dia Calhoun Repetition Reinforces The Message

Dia Calhoun has been a freelance letter-ing artist for ten years. A graduate of Mills College (Phi Beta Kappa), who also attended the Art Center College of Design, Calhoun does lettering both by hand and on the Macintosh or, as her letterhead says, "by pen or mouse." Although she is a one-person studio, she does occasionally use part-time help.

Most lettering artists send out a sin-gle sheet that shows the variety of styles in which they work. Often the sheets simply look cluttered, and the viewer's eye can't focus on any single piece of lettering—the result is discordant, visual noise. For her self-promotion, Calhoun decided to send out a series of elegantly designed cards that featured one lettering style per card. She felt this approach would not only best showcase her work but also make her promotions stand out from the crowd.

Although each card features a dif-ferent lettering style, all use the same background graphic, color scheme, paper and format to tie them together and to reinforce her studio's identity. Each art director or designer receives a group of three cards every three months for nine months. Calhoun develops a new set of cards every year for this ongoing promotion. She would like to get more book cover and theater work, because she "likes the more dramatic solutions and cre-ative freedom," so she especially tar-gets art directors and publishing houses and the appropriate people

with theater groups.

Calhoun includes pieces done for clients in order to establish her credi-bility, but she also includes pieces she has done for herself. These pieces show the kind of work she would like to get—rather than what she has already been doing. Two cards, "Sword of Faranor" and "Rapunzel," generated interesting assignments.

Each group of three is mailed in a coordinating envelope with Calhoun's signature script initial *D* and the return address. The type for the return address on the cards and the envelopes was set in Aldus PageMaker. The type and lettering echo the design of her business card, shown on this page. The coordinating paper, colors and layout of the enve-lope were carefully planned, too. Calhoun says, "It had to be interesting to get art directors to open it."

Originally, Calhoun had the cards printed three at a time, but she found it more cost effective to print nine at a time. The cards are done as a two-color offset job, using a screen of the PMS color for the background script. She had experimented with laser printing the lettering art but found that the quality and durability suffered — serious problems for timeless pieces that could be kept on file by the recipients.

The response to the mailing has been fantastic. The initial group of cards paid for itself in the second month and is still bringing in work a year-and-a-half later.

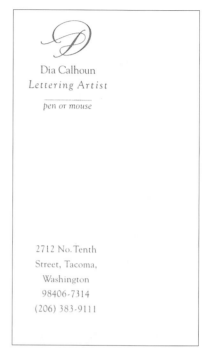

Business Card
Design: Dia Calhoun
Lettering: Dia Calhoun
The look of this business card was used as the basis for the promotional card series that Calhoun creat-ed to showcase her various lettering styles.

Card Series
Design: Dia Calhoun
Lettering: Dia Calhoun
Quantity: 2,000 each of 9 sets; total 18,000 pieces
Budget: $1,750, includ-ing envelopes
The cards are printed on Baronial Ivory Classic Crest and are mailed in a coordinat-ing green-gray Environment Wove Cypress. Calhoun con-tinues to send art direc-tors and designers one group of three cards every three months.

Alexander Isley Design Multiple Exposure

Alexander Isley Design was founded in 1988. Prior to establishing his firm, Isley held the position of senior designer at M&Co., then served as the first full-time art director of SPY *magazine. While at* SPY, *he was awarded gold and silver medals by the Society of Publication Designers. Isley has been an adjunct professor at Cooper Union and the School of Visual Arts in New York City, teaching courses in design and typography. He has spoken on design and moderated symposia before numerous professional organizations, including AIGA and the Society of Publication Designers. The studio has produced award-winning work for a diverse group of clients, including Time Warner, Nickelodeon, MTV, Giorgio Armani, WH Smith Ltd., the Rock and Roll Hall of Fame and Museum, Steelcase, Inc., Warner Bros., Pepsico and Canon USA.*

Alexander Isley doesn't do a lot of self-promotion pieces, but that doesn't mean he's unconcerned with promoting himself. His self-promotion efforts include giving talks, entering select competitions, and arranging to have the studio's work appear in design publications and journals. All of these methods stop short of "cold-calling," and the effect is cumulative. Because of these efforts, he can now rely on word of mouth for new clients. His always varied, and now quite extensive list, gives referrals the growth power of a snowball rolling down a large hill. (Just as an example of the depth of this list, he currently numbers thirty-two book and magazine publishers among present and former clients.)

When he does do self-promotion pieces, however, his distinctive visual/verbal logo often plays a key role in the design.

There isn't usually a holiday promotion from Alexander Isley Design, but it seemed appropriate to do one in conjunction with the studio's seventh anniversary in 1994. Isley had recently completed the design of an art book, *Blue Dog*, that featured the well-known Blue Dog paintings of George Rodrigue and thought it would make a nice gift. He bought enough books to send to clients and friends, then each book was wrapped in a T-shirt that had the studio's logo on the front, and "Celebrating Seven Years of Excellance" on the back. Isley intentionally misspelled "excellence," but few people got the joke. He says they figured he just didn't know how to spell.

Isley is frequently invited to speak to graphic and other arts organizations around the country. He donates his time, and asks in return that the organization print a poster of his design. He requests a minimum of two colors but may have more to work with if a printer donates services. When Isley addressed the Dallas Society of Visual Communications, the printer agreed to donate six-color printing. That poster, "The Many Faces of Alexander Isley Design," acts as a portfolio-at-a-glance, featuring a wide range of Isley's work that fits the theme of the poster. He requested overruns of the posters and mailed them to clients and prospects. The "AI in IA" poster uses the type from the studio's identity system as part of a visual anagram.

AI T-Shirt
Designer: Alexander Isley
Quantity: 200
Budget: Moderate
This T-shirt, featuring the studio's logo on the front, was sent to clients as a thank-you gift during the 1994 holiday season to celebrate the studio's seventh anniversary. Isley did intentionally misspell "excellence" in the "Celebrating Seven Years of Excellance" that appears on the back of the shirt, but he says that few people got the joke. (They must have figured he just didn't know how to spell.) The T-shirt was wrapped around a book, *Blue Dog*, that Isley Design had recently designed.

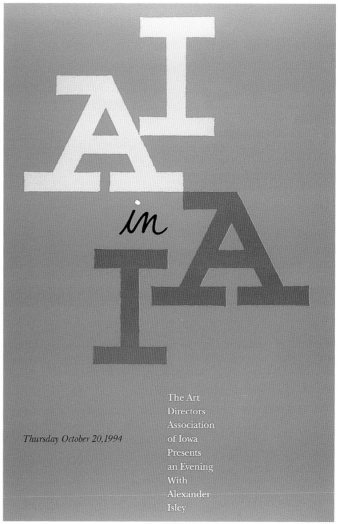

The Many Faces of Alexander Isley Design Poster

Design: Alexander Isley
Quantity: 800
Budget: Donated

This poster, designed for a talk for the Dallas Society of Visual Communications, illustrates the diversity of Isley's work. His strict adherence to the theme of the poster in his choice of visuals (all show faces, from the literal to the abstract) gives the piece continuity; in this case the whole has been made greater than the sum of its parts. He also used his overruns of this mini-portfolio in a mailing.

AI in IA Poster

Design: Alexander Isley
Quantity: 500
Budget: Design donated

Alexander Isley designed this poster as part of his arrangement to address the Art Directors Association of Iowa. The paper company that co-sponsored the talk ran the poster on several different sheets. Isley received overruns, which he sent out to a few clients and prospects. This poster illustrates the versatility as well as the strong visual appeal of Isley's identity; by substituting a capital *I* for the "eye" he normally uses, he was able to play on the abbreviation of Iowa (IA).

Sommese Design Possibilities, Not Limitations

Lanny and Kristin Sommese are husband-and-wife partners in Sommese Design in State College, Pennsylvania. They also both teach graphic design at Penn State University. Assisted by occasional free-lancers, the two-person studio handles a wide variety of graphic design projects, including corporate identity design and packaging. They have clients who are part of the university, and many who aren't. Currently, their biggest client is AquaPenn Water Company for whom they do national brand packaging.

Kristin and Lanny Sommese combine careers as graphic designers and graphic design teachers in State College, Pennsylvania. They work on projects ranging from issue-related posters for on-campus organizations to corporate identity and packaging. Some projects come their way that they can't take on because of their size (a two-person studio with occasional freelance help). But Sommese says they're very happy as designers, teachers and parents of a lively, one-year-old daughter, Saige.

Although they're a small studio, they win a lot of awards in design competitions. Sommese attributes that success to their conceptual approach. As a teacher, he is aware that young designers sometimes feel they can't do great work because of budget limitations. He can often point to his own work to counter that complaint. Sommese believes his work wins awards, even when the budget is small, because judges are impressed by the idea behind the design, the design's immediacy and its appropriateness for the client. He's conscious that his role as teacher (and lecturer) brings with it a responsibility not to follow the "design trend of the month," but to take chances and push clients as far as possible within the appropriate limits for that client.

The Sommeses do a tremendous number of issue-related posters for on-campus clients, many of which are two- or three-color pieces. When asked how he feels about working without full-color available, Sommese simply replies that full color isn't

appropriate for some clients. He adds that budget constraints can force you out of your customary creative mindset, and that can be a good thing. As an example of creatively managing on a limited budget, he cites an early letterhead design that could be cut in half to become an invoice. Trimmed down again, the same letterhead became a mailing label.

This creative flexibility is still applied to Sommese Design's identity. Lanny feels that a designer doesn't

have to keep the same identity for many years. He has already extensively changed the look of his business cards and letterhead several times. If he comes up with something else he likes, he'll change it again. Sommese aims for a memorable card, which he feels is achieved through the unusual fold in the current version. Since "the nice thing about calling cards is you don't need them all at once," folding his by hand as needed poses no problems.

Sommese T-Shirts
Design: Kristin Sommese
Illustration: Kristin Sommese
Quantity: 50
Budget: $350
Kristin, Lanny and Saige Sommese model the popular T-shirts with the studio's logo. Kristin designed a mark, a typographic adaptation of their studio name. T-shirts seemed a logical vehicle because they're popular and inexpensive. They were given to clients as gifts and to students (where potential on-campus clients would see them).

**Lanny Sommese
Calling Card Series**
Design: Lanny
  Sommese
Illustration: Lanny
  Sommese
Quantity: 300
Budget: $50
Lanny Sommese is in
the unusual position of
needing three different
calling cards, one for
each aspect of his pro-
fessional life:
designer/illustrator,
educator, and the North
American correspondent
for *Novum
Gebrauchsgraphik*
magazine. However, all
three are strongly relat-
ed visually because they
represent three sides of
the same person. The
image of an abstract
human figure inter-
twining with a T-
square, originally devel-
oped for an AIGA Call-
for-Entries poster,
seemed appropriate for
Sommese the
designer/illustrator. He
then carefully adapted
the image for the other
two cards. A "hands-to-
hands" image repre-
sents the educator and a
"person-to-person"
image represents the
correspondent. All the
cards were printed in
black ink on one side of
an 8-1/2" x 11" sheet
with a paper plate at an
instant printer.
Sometimes Sommese
hands out all three
cards at once, which is
even more memorable
because of the unusual
fold.

Effective Techniques for Self-Promotion

Production costs needn't hamper your creativity as you look for opportunities to get exposure for your studio. There are lots of vehicles for self-promotion that you may want to look at — or look at again, in a different light.

The most successful vehicles reinforce and are particularly appropriate to the studio's message. If you want to position yourself to get interactive design projects, consider a disk promotion. If you want to do more packaging design, look for a unique package for your promotion. If you're just starting out, you may want several different ways to show the full range of your work. And don't discount promotional efforts that aren't typically associated with graphic design. Studios have had success with everything from press releases to gifts of handmade birdhouses.

The studios in this section share strategies that have worked for them and that you may want to incorporate — with your own creative twist, of course — into your own promotion efforts.

Barry Power Graphic Design Making Word of Mouth Work

Barry Power started Barry Power Graphic Design in 1991 as a sideline to his full-time career as an architect. He continues to work as an architect/CAD operator in San Francisco by day and freelances as a graphic designer at night. Recent projects include a logo/identity and graphics for a children's recreation center, a book cover, brochures, flyers, business cards and letterheads, invitations, greeting cards and pro bono work.

Barry Power spent ten years in architecture, interior design and planning, working on such diverse projects as high-rise buildings, theme parks, hospitals, missile launch pads and historic renovations. But in the early 1990s, construction projects—and work for architects—came to a standstill. Power had always had a passion for graphic design—with degrees in both architectural interiors and graphic design—so he started a freelance graphic design business in 1991.

Rather than launch an expensive self-promotion campaign, Power decided to make word-of-mouth an active promotional tool. He tapped into a network of acquaintances and friends for work, leads and referrals. Contacts in the architecture and interior design business proved to be good sources of work.

San Francisco is a good place for networking because it has a large community of artists and graphic designers. Power has certainly benefitted professionally from references he's gotten, but he feels that the opportunity to sustain his awareness of historical and contemporary design may be an even greater professional benefit of his choice of location. He also finds opportunities for professional growth—and leads for work—at his MacUser group and from attending local art and design shows. Power is on the mailing lists of a variety of arts organizations, which keeps him up-to-date on what's happening.

A key component of Power's word-of-mouth self-promotion efforts are his stylish, witty business cards. Each card is different, which keeps interest high for Power as well as his clients, but they show a consistent approach to communicating his message and approach to design. These business cards are not only effective communication tools, they're also quite inexpensive to produce.

Power prints the business cards on a tabletop, color ink jet printer. He prints twenty or thirty at a time on paper he buys from art supply stores and then trims them by hand. Using his own printer gives him the flexibility to change the card whenever he wants; he can also create a new business card to suit a potential client. The low costs and flexibility of tabletop printing are great advantages, but there are some disadvantages as well:

- the vegetable-based inks used in the printer fade out over time when exposed to light;
- some design competitions won't accept them;
- the lightweight art papers aren't as durable as standard card stock (which is often too thick for a tabletop printer).

For these reasons Power does suggest that clients have their cards professionally printed, but he would recommend his own approach for other freelancers. (You may also want to experiment with the wide variety of laser papers and stationery sheets available from office supply stores, specialty catalogs and stationery stores.) If you want to show a variety of styles or to develop a mini-portfolio of your work, such as logo designs, the desktop approach could be the most effective—and low-cost—option available.

Business Cards
Designer: Barry Power
Quantity: Variable (20 to 30 at a time)
Cost: Low—varies with cost of art paper and amount of ribbon used
Power printed these cards on his HP DeskWriter 550C printer. The quality does suffer a bit, but he compensates for this by choosing typefaces that hold up well and strong, but simple, graphics. Despite the lack of commercial printing, the cards' reversed type and the color gradations still work well. The illustration style used with the gradation not only effectively conveys his message, but also conceals any defects in the printing of the gradation. He uses different papers from art supply stores to add even more variety to the cards.

passion. pride. stamina. instinct.

BARRY POWER
GRAPHIC DESIGN
3921 19TH STREET
SAN FRANCISCO
CALIFORNIA 94114
TEL 415.863.5085

BARRY POWER
GRAPHIC DESIGN
3921 19TH STREET
SAN FRANCISCO
CALIFORNIA 94114

TEL 415.863.5085

BARRY POWER
GRAPHIC DESIGN
3921 19th Street
San Francisco
California 94114
tel 415.863.5085

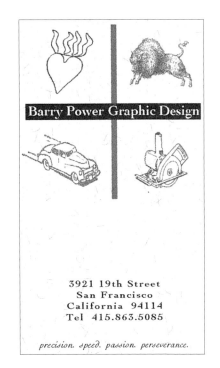

3921 19th Street
San Francisco
California 94114
Tel 415.863.5085

precision. speed. passion. perseverance.

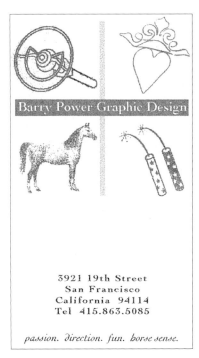

3921 19th Street
San Francisco
California 94114
Tel 415.863.5085

passion. direction. fun. horse sense.

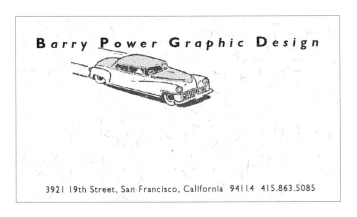

3921 19th Street, San Francisco, California 94114 415.863.5085

Abney/Huninghake Design Start Spreading the Word—Often for Free

Bruce Huninghake and his wife Karen Abney have been in business as Abney/Huninghake Design for seven years. The Louisville, Kentucky, design firm has three designers, an account representative and an office manager. Most of the staff started their careers far from Kentucky, however. Abney was a creative director of a Houston, Texas, studio before moving to Louisville, while Huninghake began his career at an ad agency in Chicago. Doreen DeHart, who handles much of the design and computer graphics responsibilities, arrived via California and Florida. Abney/Huninghake has received design awards from Print *magazine,* Art Direction *magazine, the New York Art Directors Club, the American Institute of Graphic Arts, and the Society of Illustrators.*

Karen Abney and Bruce Huninghake describe Abney/Huninghake Design as a firm that "specializes in communication through design." When it comes to their self-promotion efforts, they should perhaps change that phrase to "communication by design." They use a wide variety of vehicles including self-promotional printed pieces done both on their own and in collaboration with printers, illustrators and photographers. Although it's hard to measure a return from their pro bono work for many local and regional arts organizations, the studio believes in supporting the organizations they feel have done much for the Louisville area. And, besides the good feeling that comes from doing pro bono work, the studio gets exposure with the civic and business leaders who are active on the boards and behind the scenes of many of the arts groups.

Abney/Huninghake also uses a less common tool for graphic designers: "good, old-fashioned press releases. We have had tremendous exposure by persistently sending simple press releases to the local newspaper and business journal. The beauty of this is that it is absolutely free, and it can lead to larger stories written about you." The studio was recently listed in the local paper's "Who's Who" section, which Huninghake attributes to the frequency with which the studio's name has appeared in the papers.

According to Huninghake, there is no real "trick" to writing effective press releases, but there are some simple rules to follow:

- Send them to the media that would have the most interest in them.
- Select the media that will do you the most good.
- Make the announcement newsworthy—a new client, new staff, awards won.
- Make sure the story is succinct and timely.

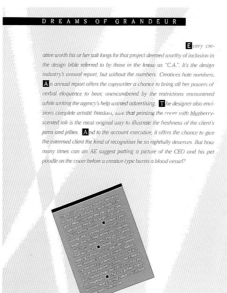

Facing the Annual Report Book
Art Direction: Karen Abney
Design: Bruce Huninghake
Illustration: Various artists
Client/Service: Scott Hull Associates
Printing: Central Printing Co.
This was a joint venture with Scott Hull (an illustrators' representative), Mead Paper and Central Printing. Everyone contributed their services and received copies of the book for promotional purposes. Scott Hull put together the deal with Mead and Central Printing, then invited Abney/Huninghake to design the "annual report." This project brought increased exposure not only from the awards it won but by being distributed by Mead through its popular Annual Report Show. It also led to a new paper promotion project from Mead.

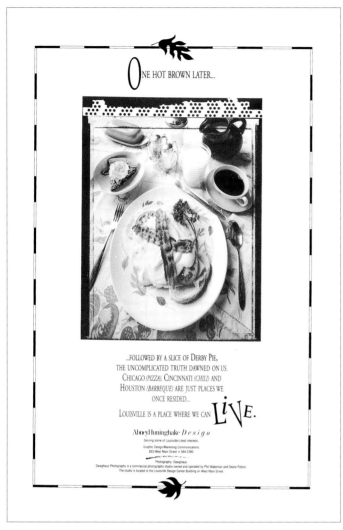

One Hot Brown Ad

Art Direction: Bruce Huninghake
Design: Karen Abney
Photography: Dawghaus Photography
Budget: $250

The *Louisville Courier Journal* offered free ad placement during a special promotion. Specifically, the paper offered a free one-week, full-page ad placement to design studios and advertising agencies that developed an ad that had something to do with the positive aspects of living and working in Louisville. The "One Hot Brown" ad, produced in collaboration with a local photographer, caught the attention of a popular local disc jockey. He liked the ad so much that he called Abney and Huninghake and conducted an on-the-air interview during his early morning show.

Postcard Set/Leave-Behind

Art Direction: Bruce Huninghake
Design: Karen Abney
Photography: Dawghaus Photography
Quantity: 500 each card
Budget: $1,500

In this postcard set, each card shows several pieces of work in a specific category — annual reports, packaging, promotions, etc. Abney/Huninghake decided this was an ideal way of getting their work in front of people, even if they couldn't get an appointment. The cards were sent out every two weeks and some were also used as leave-behinds. With only one image per card, they were relatively inexpensive, too.

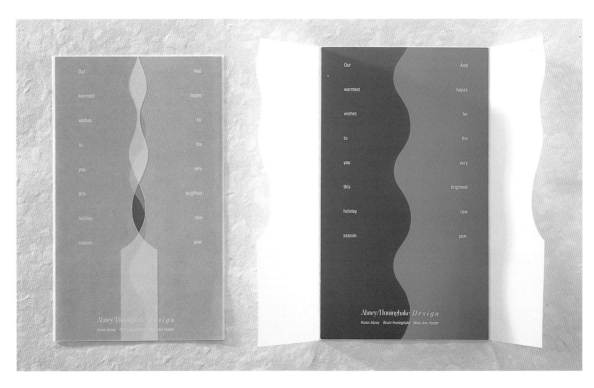

Abney/Huninghake Christmas Card

Art Direction: Karen Abney

Design: Bruce Huninghake

Quantity: 500

Budget: $500

Abney/Huninghake decided on this novelty card to have a piece that would not only stand out in a stack of mail but also get their work in front of people. The vellum "wave" on these cards was cut by hand using a template.

United Way Annual Report

Art Direction: Bruce Huninghake

Design: Bruce Huninghake

Budget: Design donated

This was a very low budget pro bono project. The studio was asked to design this annual report using existing photography. United Way had previously asked local photographers to shoot a day's worth of organizations and operations funded by the nonprofit foundation. The images were great but had already been overused in various other promotions.

Abney/Huninghake creatively cropped the images and ran color over the photos. Although the piece was actually printed 2/2 (two colors/two sides), many people thought it was a four-color job.

Nicky Ovitt Big Four-Color Look, Low Price

Nicky Ovitt lived in San Francisco for seven years and worked at Levi Strauss & Co. in mens' jeans marketing. She met Scott Idleman with whom she started Blink, a studio specializing in logos and record packaging, then moved home to New Mexico and joined the staff of Vaughn Wedeen Creative. She has now started her own business, specializing in lettering and illustration "with my ink, paint and scissors." Her client list includes Beckett Paper, Elektra Records, Gensler & Associates, Levi Strauss & Co. and Warner Bros. Records.

An illustrator who does four-color work, and wants to get more of it, has to be creative in order to keep her promotions affordable. Nicky Ovitt solved the problem by thinking small. Her compact self-mailer promo consists of four full-color postcards that can be torn off and used by the recipient. The cover, which acts as the envelope, is printed with solids and

screens of one ink color on a sturdy but inexpensive paper. The cover folds down to 5-1/2" x 7" and the whole package weighs only a couple of ounces to keep mailing costs down. The piece also can be updated easily if Ovitt moves since she adds her address and phone number in red ink to the cover.

My Name Is Nicky Postcards
Design: Nicky Ovitt, Scott Idleman
Artwork: Nicky Ovitt
Quantity: 1,000
Budget: $1,000
The four postcards are perforated so they can be torn off and used. Ovitt tapes her business card with

brightly striped tape to the postcard that shows the same image. The business card is preprinted with "Hello, My name is Nicky" in one of her lettering styles. Ovitt adds her address and phone number to both the business card and the mailer's cover in red ink.

Sayles Graphic Design Targeting Clients With Promotion

Sayles Graphic Design was founded in 1985 by designer John Sayles and former client, Sheree Clark. The two met when Clark hired Sayles for a design project at Drake University, where she then worked. They hit it off, and Clark soon left Drake for the new graphic design studio. Clark, a natural motivator and salesperson, handles many of the business aspects of the studio, allowing Sayles to do what he does best—design. The two principals have been joined by a staff of four. To date, the firm has won over 450 design awards and counts Diners Club, Saks Fifth Avenue, Nike and James River Corp. among its clients.

Sayles Graphic Design started on a shoestring with clients who didn't have major budgets. Their first job, an annual report for a nonprofit organization, had a budget of $1,000 including printing. But it did offer the fledgling firm a lot of creative freedom and attracted some favorable attention in the design press. Partners John Sayles and Sheree Clark saw an opportunity to do good *and* get the word out about the new studio, so they began building a client base of nonprofit organizations interested in exciting, and often unconventional, design work. This approach paid off: The firm received a lot of exposure—and a number of prestigious design awards—and soon was recognized as a "hot" new studio.

Long-term planning is still a key element in the studio's promotional efforts. Sayles and Clark want a greater percentage of their projects to be direct mail design in the next few years. In the studio's second decade, Sayles looks forward to exploring new areas of design, including industrial design. Clark has set a goal of expanding the studio's client base to include international clients. Sayles and Clark find that having one person concentrate on the business end while the other concentrates on design enables them to keep the quality of both design and customer service at a high level. They believe this method of running a design studio has helped set them apart in the industry.

The partners put a lot of energy into attracting the right clients and then keeping them. Clark is constantly looking for ways to draw these clients. She believes that getting recognition for the studio in the media and through contests is still a critical part of their self-promotion. So, she responds to many calls for entries (and is as helpful as possible to the organizers) and issues media releases. Because Clark and Sayles would like to get more direct mail projects, they have begun to target appropriate clients through both a traditional printed promotion and an unusual vehicle—authoring a book on the subject. Clark and Wendy Lyons, the studio's copywriter, wrote a book titled *Creative Direct Mail Design: The Guide and Showcase*. After the book's publication, the studio sent out the attention-getting "we wrote the book on direct mail" promotion. Clark hopes the book will help establish the studio's credibility in the area of direct mail, an image that can then be reinforced by the direct mail package. Clark is now at work on a second book, *Great Design Using Non-Traditional Materials* (North Light Books), that draws on the studio's well-known expertise with materials such as acrylics, wood, metal and chipboard in unusual applications such as direct mail, brochures and collateral.

We Draw Circles Around the Rest Promotion
Art Direction: John Sayles
Design: John Sayles
Illustration: John Sayles
Quantity: 1,250
Budget: Under $3 each
A good self-promotion gives the client a taste of what it's like to do business with the studio. This triangular box is printed with bright graphics and contains a toy top with a felt-tip pen. Recipients spin the top and watch it draw spirals, thereby graphically illustrating the piece's headline, "Sayles Graphic Design Draws Circles Around the Rest!" Clark says, "Clients tell me they love the top and can't stop playing with it."

**John Sayles
Makes his Marks
Logo Book**

Art Direction: John
 Sayles
Design: John Sayles
Illustration: John
 Sayles
Quantity: 250
Budget: Under $3 each
This spiral-bound book
was printed in one
color. Sayles and Clark
use it in response to
requests from business-
es and organizations for
samples of the firm's
corporate identity work.

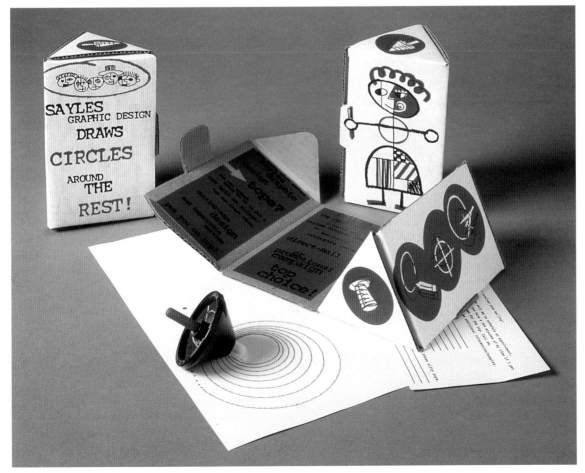

**Tip Top Design
T-Shirt**

Art Direction: John
    Sayles
Design: John Sayles
Illustration: John
    Sayles
Quantity: 36
Budget: Approximately
    $10 each

9 Years T-Shirt

Art Direction: John
    Sayles
Design: John Sayles
Illustration: John
    Sayles
Quantity: 36
Budget: Approximately
    $10 each

Sayles Graphic Design is well known for the striking T-shirts they've designed over the years. At least once a year, the studio designs and produces a "limited edition" T-shirt. The shirts are not intended to attract new clients, but rather to thank vendors, staff, and a few of their current clients. Sayles and Clark feel that maintaining relationships with vendors is just as important as maintaining good client service. It's a wise practice and one too many designers overlook, but vendors can be a valuable source of referrals and leads as well as quality service. Printing only a small quantity increases the value to the recipient and helps keep costs reasonable.

"We Wrote the Book on Direct Mail"
Promotion

Art Direction: John Sayles
Design: John Sayles
Illustration: John Sayles
Quantity: 1,500
Budget: Under $3 each

Many of the studio's promotions are built around a strong theme that is then translated by a punchy headline and powerful graphics. For this promotion, an old cliche is given a new slant with a surprising, literal interpretation. The bold package was designed to toot Sayles' horn *and* to promote the book on direct mail design that Clark co-authored with Wendy Lyons, the studio's copywriter.

A Time to Remember Poster

Art Direction: John Sayles
Design: John Sayles
Illustration: John Sayles
Quantity: 100
Budget: Less than $3 each

Done in collaboration with a screen printer, this poster served as a holiday greeting. Both the design firm and the printer used the greeting, with each providing services to the other as a trade arrangement. To avoid duplication, the two organizations compared lists of poster recipients.

John DeSantis Building Your Freelance Business

John DeSantis works full-time producing promotions and marketing materials for the Graphic Presentation Unit of the United Nations Postal Administration (UNPA). He creates ads, publications, presentations, logos and direct marketing materials for the New York, Geneva and Vienna UNPA offices. He also works with renowned artists, illustrators and designers to create artwork suitable for postage stamps. Although working full-time, he continues to freelance on the side.

John DeSantis's extensive work experience at several publishing companies provided him with some valuable ideas for promoting the freelance business he maintains in addition to his full-time job with the UNPA. Time to design, much less promote himself, is definitely at a premium if DeSantis wants to eat, sleep and have any personal life at all. So, every promotion must be carefully planned and produce good results.

Always savvy about promotion, DeSantis spent "about two hundred dollars" on a mailing list from a mailing label company for one of his early promotions. Lists vary in price, but they generally cost at least two hundred dollars, depending on how many qualifiers you want (i.e., how closely you want to target your audience). He targeted publishers with his "Designer's Profile" package (shown on the facing page) — a resume is printed on the back of the "Designer's Profile" piece, which he then poly-bagged with a business card, a business reply card and some samples of his work. The resume emphasizes his publication experience and computer skills.

New York City is a very competitive market for creative professionals. DeSantis networks and promotes himself to bring in work he enjoys pursuing on his own time. He belongs to AIGA, the Advertising Club of New York, and the Graphic Artist's Guild. Because of his interest in art, music and Italian culture, DeSantis actively solicits work, much of it pro bono, from organizations in those fields. This work gives him a chance to take on challenging projects that are often more interesting than the work that pays the bills.

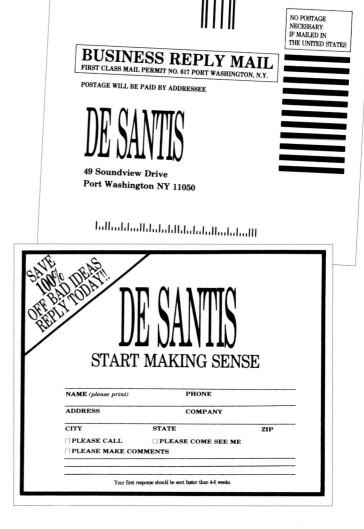

Business Card
Art Direction: John DeSantis
Design: John DeSantis
Illustration: John DeSantis
DeSantis' business card was packaged along with his resume (printed on the back of the "Designer's Profile" sheet), a business reply card and some samples of his work.

Business Reply Card
Art Direction: John DeSantis
Design: John DeSantis
Budget: $150
DeSantis had designed many business reply cards (BRCs) while working for a computer publisher, so he went to the post office to learn how to do one for himself. For a fifty dollar fee he received a permit number. He was charged forty cents for each card returned; the post office billed him monthly.

Color Photocopies

Art Direction: John DeSantis

Design: John DeSantis

Quantity: Small batches, varies

Budget: Moderate, varies with number run

Making color photocopies of his work lets DeSantis enclose appropriate samples targeted to each client or potential client in a mailing. That way, he never runs out of samples of a particular piece and can quickly update his portfolio with new work. These two pieces are projects DeSantis did for Italian cultural organizations. "Lapolla," a poster for interior design, is displayed in showrooms.

DeSantis Puzzle

Art Direction: John DeSantis

Design: John DeSantis

Quantity: Approximately 10

Budget: Low (used many materials on hand)

Although DeSantis came up with the concept for this promotion piece in school, he didn't produce it for several years. He applied his logo to an electronic puzzle for the Macintosh where a face or numbers can be reconfigured on the screen. DeSantis made color photocopies of the result and mounted them on two thicknesses of foamcore board. He set up a jig to cut out the pieces which could then slide around in the slots. He only manufactured about ten puzzles because they were so labor intensive, but he received a response from everyone who got the puzzle.

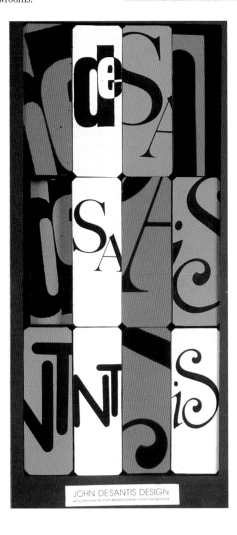

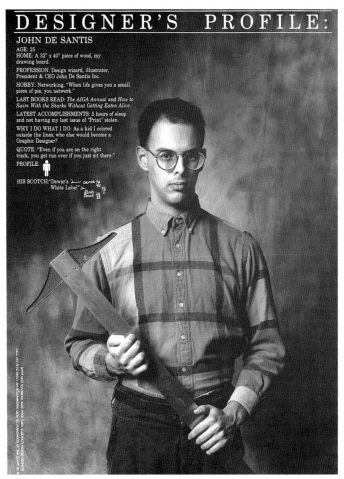

Designer's Profile

Art Direction: John DeSantis

Design: John DeSantis

Budget: $500

DeSantis wanted to show a sample of his work and have a more interesting visual than would be possible with a standard resume. The profile was printed 2/2 (two colors/two sides) on stock the printer had left over from another job. DeSantis polybagged the package by hand, inserting a copy of the profile, his business card, a BRC, and samples of his work for a mailing to publishing houses.

Studio MD Interactive Portfolio on a Disk

Studio MD in Seattle specializes in computer-generated design. Founded in 1989 by Glen Paul Mitsui and Jesse Doquilo, and later joined by Randy Lim, the studio has applied its classical and electronic design expertise to a wide range of projects for a diverse group of clients: corporate, business and high technology leaders, innovative start-up companies, art showcases and museum exhibitions. The studio has also done pro bono work for a number of worthy causes. Their client list includes Apple Computer, Microsoft Inc., Seattle Medical Systems Group, Entertainment Weekly, Newsweek, Time, *Nissan/Infiniti, the Port of Seattle, Seattle Aquarium and the United Way. The trio has received numerous local and national awards for their print designs, computer-based designs, and digital illustrations, including publication in* Graphis, Print, HOW *and* Communication Arts *magazines.*

Studio MD's Glen Mitsui, Jesse Doquilo and Randy Lim are counted among the pioneers of computer-generated design and illustration.

Their hybrid, classical-hypermodern approach attempts to combine the best of both traditional design concepts and techniques and those developed from modern technology. The firm's trademark is a multi-dimensional style of graphic art described as "interactive print design." The term arises from the high degree of personal involvement that the print work has with its audience. This interaction is encouraged by the ingeniously configured, multifaceted shape and fold of the work and the richly detailed content of the illustrations.

Among their major achievements, Studio MD counts its cosmetic ski designs for PRE of Utah and the 1992 holiday decorations displayed at the Seattle-Tacoma (Sea-Tac) International Airport. Their digital illustrations have appeared on the covers of the *1992 HOW Business Annual, MacWorld, PC World* and *Publish* as well as in a series of promotional materials for Nissan/Infiniti.

Recognized by the design and computer development industries for their pioneering efforts, Mitsui and Doquilo are now asked to share their expertise with others, lecturing to both design and computer professionals across the country. In order to demonstrate and promote their computer talents to clients in other industries, they have chosen an interactive presentation of their talents.

Although the portfolio on a disk is becoming more common as clients computerize, Studio MD has relied on theirs for several years now. It's an excellent example of showing the kind of work you want to get more of. The interactive portfolio on disk has been well received by clients, generating a lot of multimedia assignments. The designers manage to involve the viewer in the presentation and to communicate a sense of the fun they have with their work. The irreverent, humorous personality of the studio comes through as a background to the portfolio of work.

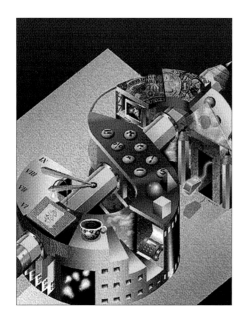  

Studio MD Interactive Portfolio Disk
Art Direction: Glenn Mitsui, Randy Lim, Jesse Doquilo
Design: Glenn Mitsui
Production: Glenn Mitsui
Quantity: As needed

Budget: Low; varies with cost of box of diskettes
The interactive portfolio program was scripted with Macromind Director. Background sounds include footsteps, traffic and Mitsui humming. (He wasn't sure about music copyrights, so he simply hummed as a background.)

Studio MD Disk Labels

Art Direction: Glenn Mitsui, Randy Lim, Jesse Doquilo
Design: Glenn Mitsui
Illustration: Glenn Mitsui
Quantity: 750
Budget: $653

These labels, created in Adobe Photoshop, allowed Mitsui to experiment a lot on a project without a real deadline. A creature of habit, he still knocked out the fifteen ideas shown on this sheet in a couple of days.

Disk Labels in use
Two of the Studio MD disk labels in use.

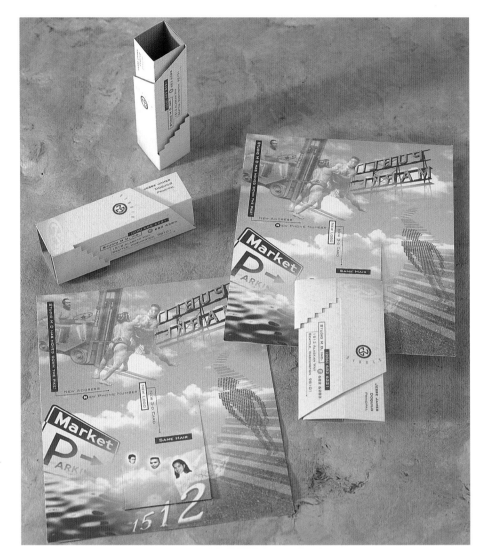

Studio MD Moving Announcement

Art Direction: Jesse Doquilo, Randy Lim,
    Glenn Mitsui

Design: Jesse Doquilo

Photography: Jesse Doquilo

Illustration: Jesse Doquilo

Quantity: 500

Budget: $85 using existing business cards (sixteen
    cents each)

This announcement was designed to showcase the
business card inserted in a hand die-cut opening.
The announcement is a one-color job that comple-
ments the card with whimsical images designed in
Adobe Photoshop. The theme, "new address . . .
same hair," lets the recipient know the designers
have fun with their image and don't take themselves too seriously.

Lim Baby Announcement

Art Direction: Randy Lim

Design: Randy and Elana Lim

Photography: Randy Lim

Quantity: 250

Budget: $150

Produced for family and friends, this announcement
is quite a contrast with the studio's high-tech
imagery. The leaf is made from torn bark paper purchased at an art supply store. The limb is a real twig.

Studio MD Handmade Book

Art Direction: Jesse Doquilo, Randy Lim, Glenn
    Mitsui

Design: Jesse Doquilo

Quantity: 100

Budget: $3 each

These books, made mainly from recycled office
materials, show the softer side of the studio. Since
most of Studio MD's work is done on the computer,
this project gave them a chance to do something
very tactile. Scraps of flooring, popcorn wrappers
and a variety of other materials are assembled into
books that Doquilo says are almost too precious to
part with. They do only two or three at a time, as
needed, in order not to burn out on the production.

Jon Flaming Design Great Gifts Build Business

Jon Flaming Design is a design and illustration studio in Dallas, working on corporate identity, packaging, retail design, poster design and illustration. Flaming is a former member of the board of directors for the Texas chapter of the American Institute of Graphic Arts. He recently went with a national rep based in Dallas for his illustration work. Clients include American Way Magazine, *The Dallas Zoo, Ericsson,* JCPenney, Motorola, Neiman Marcus, *PespsiCo and the Rouse Company. The studio's work has appeared in* Communication Arts, Graphis, Print, HOW, *the* Society of Publication Designers Annual, *the* Society of Illustrators Annual, *the* American Illustration Annual, *the* New York Art Directors Club Show, and the Mead Top 60 Show.

Jon Flaming started his own studio two and a half years ago and divides his time equally between design and illustration. Unless a design project calls for a photograph, Flaming tries to find a way to do the illustration himself. Some clients hire him for his illustration style, then find out he can handle the design. He does all the ads and catalogs for a retail client in New York, who knows his illustration style and is happy that he can handle entire projects himself. Although he likes to be in control of the entire project, he also works as an illustrator for art directors.

Flaming does a variety of promotions, but his current and prospective clients are always excited by the wonderful three-dimensional gifts and T-shirts they sometimes receive. Flaming's T-shirt designs are so popular that he found a market for them in a Dallas card and gift shop. Ken Knight, the store's owner, buys enough T-shirts to cover Flaming's cost to produce them. The other T-shirts are given to clients as much-appreciated "thank you" gifts.

Many of the three-dimensional items come from Flaming's home woodworking shop, but he can't find as much time for his hobby as he would like with two small children (a two-year-old and a three-year-old) and one on the way. Flaming began

making clocks and birdhouses as one-of-a-kind gifts for clients and professional contacts. These unique objects were so well received that he and a partner have formed a second business, called Objex, to market them.

People Promotion
Design: Jon Flaming
Illustration: Jon Flaming
Quantity: As needed
This is the first in a series of promotional pieces. The second, already in the works, will be called "Things." This sheet was run on a good photocopier on a good laser stock, and mailed with a piece of card stock in a 9" x 12" envelope. Primarily intended to keep current clients up-to-date, it is also mailed to a few potential clients.

**Moving
Announcement (With
Business Card)**
Design: Jon Flaming
Illustration: Jon
    Flaming
Quantity: 300
Budget: $250
Flaming wanted to
design a practical, func-
tional moving
announcement. The
mover "holds"
Flaming's business
cards in his die-cut
hands, adding a three-
dimensional quality to
the piece while making
it easy for the recipient
to add the card to a
Rolodex or file. Printed
black on Evergreen
Kraft by Simpson, the
piece has a gritty, pack-
ing material look
against which the busi-
ness card, printed on
Star White from
Vicksburg, stands out
sharply.

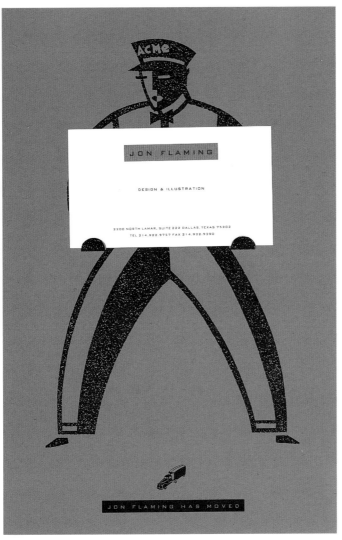

**Heart of Rock and
Roll Poster**
Design: Jon Flaming
Illustration: Jon
    Flaming
This poster was done for
a fund-raiser for the
American Heart
Association. The project
also includes an invita-
tion and a T-shirt.
Flaming was
approached on behalf
of the American Heart
Association by a woman
who admires his work.
The project was ideal
because Flaming was
given complete artistic
freedom. He wanted to
do a silkscreened poster,
and his contact
arranged to have the
printing donated.

Illustration Promo
Design: Jon Flaming
Illustration: Jon Flaming
Quantity: As needed
Cost: Very low, varies with number of photocopies.
Flaming designed this promo when he signed with
a national rep. He doesn't feel his style is compro-
mised by running these pieces on a color photocopi-
er; in fact, the work is sometimes enhanced.
Flaming feels the promo "lets the work speak for
itself."

KNIGHT READING

KEN KNIGHT
DALLAS

ROMANTIC KNIGHT

KEN KNIGHT
DALLAS

KNIGHT VISION

KEN KNIGHT
DALLAS

Ken Knight Promo Cards
Design: Jon Flaming
Illustration: Jon Flaming
Ken Knight has what Flaming describes as "the neatest card and gift shop in Dallas." Flaming did these promo cards on a very low budget for Knight and received overruns for his own promotion.

Square Dancer, Zookeepers and Cowboy Jake T-Shirts
Design: Jon Flaming
Illustration: Jon Flaming
Quantity: Variable
Budget: $4.50 to $5 per shirt; costs covered by sale
Ken Knight purchases enough T-shirts for his store to cover Flaming's production costs, about $4.50 per shirt for one to four colors and $5 per shirt for five or six colors. Flaming gives the shirts as "thank you" gifts to clients; they are strictly promotional for him. "You don't make a lot of money on T-shirts unless you come up with a design everybody wants." Still, he enjoys the complete freedom he has in designing them.

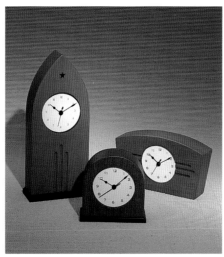

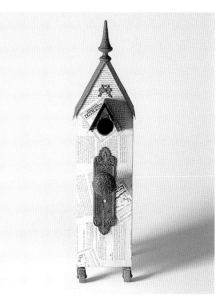

Objects

Design: Jon Flaming
Construction: Jon Flaming
Quantity: Variable
Budget: Low; varies with piece and quantity

Flaming began making clocks and birdhouses as unique gifts for clients and professional contacts. The gifts proved so popular that he and a partner have formed a business called Objex to market them. The clocks are made of wood or construction board and handmade paper. He gets the clock works from craft stores and has found an outlet in San Francisco for "neat hands." The birdhouses are constructed from objects Flaming finds out in the Texas countryside, including tin off old barns and old door knobs. There are four sizes of journals. He produced 150 of each size, working with a local binder using scrap paper. Flaming applies various icons from old jobs with heavy-duty spray mount. He took the journals to a show in San Francisco and is still filling orders from that one show.

Adams Photography Campaigning for the Right Clients

Lisa Adams was majoring in Industrial Arts at Appalachian State University when she began to develop her own dramatic style of photography. "Light is everything," she says. "It adds feeling and emotion. It dramatizes." Charlotte, North Carolina, provides her with an ideal setting for Adams Photography. The city is growing, and it is located near many other towns that can provide work. Adams specializes in photography for brochures, annual reports, print ads and specialty catalogs.

Many creative professionals have enough work to support themselves, but it's not creatively satisfying. When you reach that point, a carefully crafted self-promotion campaign can get—and keep—your name in front of the kinds of clients you want (rather than those you have to put up with).

Lisa Adams's photography studio is based where she can find a lot of work. She pulls clients not only from Charlotte, North Carolina, where her studio is located, but also from towns in a larger area, such as Spartanburg and Greenville, South Carolina. These towns are large enough to support a couple of good shooters, but the advertising agencies often have more work than the local photographers can handle.

Adams knows the kind of work she prefers to get. "I aspire to do work that has a question mark behind it, where everyone is willing to take a risk and go out on a limb. I like it when art directors come in and have an idea of what they want, but want me to help them complete the circle. I want to give something to the job creatively."

In order to find and promote her-self to the kind of art directors and agencies that she wants to work for, Adams and her assistant comb through *Ad Week* and other publications looking for people who are doing the most exciting work. During her eleven years in business, Adams has assembled a mailing list of about 350 names. Once she had the right names, all that remained was to find the right promotion to attract their attention.

For her tenth anniversary, Adams tried mailing out a portfolio on disk. Clients told her they loved the piece, but it wasn't very practical for them. They wanted something they could review without having to shut down whatever they were doing on the computer, something they could put in a file and then show to others later. Armed with that information, Adams approached Charlotte designer Mervil Paylor and copywriter Melissa Stone for a new promotion piece. This collaboration produced a package that even top creative professionals couldn't ignore.

The new campaign was beautiful and intriguing—and it could easily be stored and shown to others. Approximately every eight days, the recipient received a component of the campaign, which was produced to maximize efficiency in printing. Many materials were effectively reused from one phase to the next. A dozen photo sheets reappear later as postcards. File folders become a book cover and dividers. Copy was printed on labels for two applications rather than being printed twice.

- *Mailer #1*: This package held a jagged-edge file folder, business card, and three photo sheets (shoes, aspirin and marbles). Each image was accompanied by a provocative quotation that fit the "Stop the Eye" theme of the promotion. It was mailed in a chip-board envelope with the 8-1/2" x 11" "Eve" image from Adams' identity applied to the front. The open area in the center of the image was large enough to accommodate a mailing label for the address. The file folder was later trimmed to make the cover for a spiral-bound book containing all the images eventually used in the campaign. A label with the main promotional copy for the piece was fixed to the front of the file folder; it would later also be applied to the book cover.

- *Mailer #2*: Mailed in a white envelope with the Adams Photography mailing label, this contained a booklet with different copy that again picked up the theme of the enclosed photo sheets—coffee cup, forks, papaya.

- *Mailer #3*: The package was made up of the same elements as the second mailer, but the theme for this copy and set of photo sheets was beautiful people—a man's back, a woman with a monocle, an old woman.

- *Mailer #4*: The last package changed to the theme, "Objects of Desire" and included photo sheets showing a car, tubes and a fan.

- *Mailer #5*: The photo sheets from the first four mailers now reap-peared as a dozen postcards accompanied by a thank-you note printed on chipboard. The bundle was tied with a black ribbon and included a business card.

Adams Photography Campaign

Photography: Lisa R. Adams

Design: Mervil M. Paylor

Copywriting: Melissa Stone

Quantity: 500 - 2,000

Printing Cost: $9,729

Designer Mervil Paylor, who worked for trade, developed a campaign that created impact and reinforced Adams' identity. The promotion was divided into separate pieces that would be mailed roughly every week to ten days for five weeks. The continuing two-color design, based on the Adams Photography identity system Paylor had designed for her, tied the pieces to each other and to the studio's identity. It also somewhat offset the necessary expense of printing some photo sheets in full color. In response to her clients' suggestion that any promotion be easily filed, Adams provided a folder that would also stand out in any drawer.

GROOMING THE PRINTER®

a true story

(as best can be remembered)

Tharp Did It (T. Rick Tharp's (RT) design firm, received a phone call at 9:15AM Monday, July 6, 1992, from Acme Business Cards, Inc. (ABC; a fictitious name, used to protect the true identity of a printer in the San Francisco Bay Area).

ring . . . . ring . . .

T: 'cool morning. Tharp Did It.

ABC: Oh . . . that's cute. (giggle) This is Adrianne (real name) from Acme Business Cards. Is Rick Tharp there?

T: That's Tharp. One moment please.

RT: Rick here.

ABC: (another giggle) This is Adrianne from Acme Business Cards and I'm calling about an order we received from you today.

RT: Oh . . . yes.

ABC: We have a few details we'd like to go over with you. Do you have a second?

RT: Yes I do.

ABC: First . . . today is Monday and you've ordered Red and Black engraved business cards?

RT: Yes I did. Those are my favorite colors.

ABC: Well, Mondays are Blue.

RT: You're telling me!

ABC: (giggle) No sir. I don't think you understand. I mean: we only run Red ink on Wednesdays and Blue on Mondays. So, we won't be able to deliver your cards to you on our regular 24-hour turnaround.

RT: Today is Blue? When did you say Red is?

ABC: Wednesday.

RT: Can you hold the order until Wednesday?

RT: If that's good for you, it's OK with me. A couple more days won't make much difference. But I do have a question about your printing process. You said your cards are engraved, but the samples in your catalogue are thermographed.

ABC: Well . . . yes, that's right. We call it engraving but it's really thermography. Most of our customers don't know the difference so it's just better for us to call it engraving.

RT: I'm sure it is.

ABC: Well, our prices are very competitive when compared to actual engraving.

RT: I thought it was something like that when I saw your price was only $28 for 500 cards.

ABC: Can I turn you over to our printing department? They've got a question about the paper you've selected.

RT: Sure.

ABC: Mr. Carp?

ABC: Your order says you'd like us to use Simpson Evergreen paper for your business cards. Considering the Red and Black ink you selected, we think a paper that's a bit lighter than the dark pink would make the card more readable. Evergreen has little fibers in it and Red probably won't show up as well as it would on something like our Canary Yellow.

RT: You are probably right about that Canary, but I like the idea of using recycled paper. Besides, I heard that the little grey fibers are actually recycled poodle trimmings mixed into the paper.

ABC: We buy our paper direct from a merchant house and aren't aware of the process used for getting those fibers into the paper, but, I don't think it's made from poodle hairs, Mr. Carp.

RT: I'd still like the paper anyway.

ABC: Alright, we can do whatever you want. We keep it in stock so, it's no problem. We just wanted to check with you before we went any further with the order. But, I would like to transfer you to our art department. They have a question about the logos you've selected. Can you hold while I transfer you?

RT: Sure.

ABC: Hello, Mr. Harp?

RT: That's Tharp.

ABC: We want to make sure the logos you've chosen from our catalogue are the ones you want on your business card. You picked number 272 and number 227.

RT: I'm sorry. I don't have your catalogue in front of me. Could you tell me what the images are?

ABC: Yes. Number 272 is a poodle and number 227 is a chain saw.

RT: That's correct. That is what I specified.

ABC: Oh, then you must want two different business cards. One for your kennel business and one for your firewood business?

RT: No. They both go on the same card. If you read the text you'll see that . . .

ABC: I'm sorry Sir, but our typesetting is done in another department so we don't have access to the text here. I'm going to switch you over to them. Maybe they can straighten this out. If you could hold for just a minute, I'll connect you with them.

RT: Sure. I'm not too busy today anyway.

ABC: Mr. Tharp?

RT: Yes, it's still me.

ABC: Did you place an order for the poodle grooming card with illustration number 272?

RT: Yes I did.

ABC: I'd like to make a recommendation regarding the lettering style you've selected.

RT: OK.

ABC: You selected HI752 for the business name Tharp Did It. That typeface doesn't really reflect the business you're in and we thought you might want to consider something with a little more style and flair.

RT: Is HI752 Helvetica?

ABC: Why, yes it is.

RT: Do you have Helvetica Swash?

ABC: No, I don't think we have that one, but we're ordering some new styles in a while and that might be one of them. Would you like for me to ask our order department to hold your order?

RT: No, that's alright. I really don't want to wait.

ABC: Oh, it won't take long.

RT: No, I mean I don't want to hold up the printing of the cards until you get the new style ordered. Do you have another suggestion?

ABC: Perhaps something like PA562 would . . .

RT: I don't have your catalogue in front of me. Could you tell me what PA whatever it is looks like?

ABC: It's PA562 and it's a script with a little flair to it. I think it would be more appropriate, considering the business you're in.

RT: You're the pros. If you think it would be better, then it's OK with me.

ABC: We'll get the order going right away. I'll let me transfer you to Adrianne in our order office. She needs to talk to you for a second.

RT: Sure. I've got most of the morning.

ABC: Rick?

RT: Yes?

ABC: We won't be able to get the changes to you until next week because of all the . . .

RT: Changes? What changes? You are only changing a typeface and the card hasn't even been typeset yet? I could really use some cards this weekend at an AIGA event I'll be . . .

ABC: A what?

RT: An A. I. G. A. . . . . Oh, never mind. Next week will be fine. Thanks for calling.

ABC: You're welcome Mr. Tharp. Oh, yes, just one more thing.

About that chain saw . . .

WARNING: We the enemy and the enemv and

ART DIRECTION

12 noon, Thursday, July 16, 1992

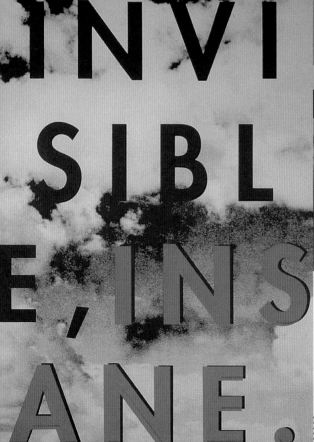

INVISIBLE, INSANE.

Gone...out of sight, out of mind.

RICK WAS BORN IN 1952 IN MANSFIELD, OHIO. THEN HE WENT TO COLLEGE AT MIAMI UNIVERSITY (NOT IN FLORIDA). AND AFTER THAT HE CAME TO CALIFORNIA AND OPENED A SMALL DESIGN FIRM CALLED THARP DID IT. HE NOW HAS SIX OTHERS DOING IT WITH HIM. SOME WIN AWARDS CERTIFICATES FOR THE STUFF THEY DO, (USUALLY NOT ON A COMPUTER). THEM ON A CLOTHESLINE ACROSS THE WON A CLIO ONCE, BUT CAN'T FIND LIKES TO DO NON-CORPORATE IDENTITY AND POSTERS THAT GET INTO THE U.S.LIBRARY OF CONGRESS. BIG STUFF TOO. LI DISLIKES SOFTWARE OUPLE HER O TH A E D HI

ANNUAL REPORT

Part Three

Getting a Response With Wit and Humor

Humorous or witty promotions can have a huge impact on clients, but it's important that you know your audience. Many of the promotions in this section, for example, were primarily targeting other creative professionals. So it was appropriate to take chances that might not have paid off with a more general audience.

Nonetheless, if you want to be a part of the creative process with your clients, and not just brought in at the last minute to style the type, you need to show clients how you think.

Humorous campaigns are memorable and often provide great word-of-mouth benefits. You presume a certain familiarity and like-mindedness with the recipient of a humorous campaign, and when it works, you've definitely broken the ice.

Graphik On!on Provoking a Reaction

Tom Slayton and David Cuccio started Graphik On!on in Columbus, Ohio, in 1989 on a shoestring budget with only a couple of clients. The firm now employs six people, including an office manager and a designer with computer graphics experience. The studio, which moved from its humble space on the outskirts of Columbus to grander space downtown in 1994, has built a successful niche creating internal work for clients such as manufacturers, banks, restaurants and law firms. They also take on overflow work from agencies and marketing firms, visualizing ideas with marker comps.

Irreverent humor has become the hallmark of the self-promotion efforts of the Graphik On!on. This is perhaps less surprising when you consider that David Cuccio was educated at the Joe Kubert School of Cartoon and Graphic Art in Dover, New Jersey. (Tom Slayton's training in illustration was more traditional.) They met while working together on the staff of a design firm that they felt was growing too large too fast.

When they decided to start a studio together, they chose the name "Graphic Union," but some sloppy penmanship transformed the studio into "Graphik On!on," a name more in keeping with their style. Cuccio and Slayton point out that the name is also appropriate for a studio that got its start at lunch in a White Castle, a restaurant chain noted for the onions on its distinctive hamburgers.

Risk-taking humor is typical of both their promotional work and their work for clients. The studio has carved out a niche doing creative—and often zany—but appropriate internal design projects. Although their clients include many companies such as banks and law firms that project conservative images to the world, these same clients are willing to take more risks with internal work. Because it's a small shop, Graphik On!on can invest the time required to develop unique, offbeat (and frequently low budget) designs for internal promotions and publications that larger studios can't tackle with their heavier overhead.

Slayton and Cuccio also actively seek work from advertising agencies and marketing firms. One of their primary means for reaching this segment of Graphik On!on's client base has been advertising in *Adfed Advocate*, the quarterly magazine of the Advertising Federation of Columbus and Central Ohio. It's an inexpensive promotional tool; the full page black-and-white ads cost $250 to run plus their production costs.

Because the publication is circulated to other creatives, agencies and printers, Slayton and Cuccio feel they can take some risks with their humor to get attention from their audience. Usually the reaction to the ads has been positive, but one that referred to the caning of an American in Singapore was described as "sick" by a few people. They didn't decide to change their approach to promotion, though. As a friend at an agency told them, "Any reaction—good or bad—is good."

Although Cuccio and Slayton wouldn't promote themselves to the corporate community with the same kind of "shock value" humor, they feel humor can have a place in any promotional effort. (If a client has no sense of humor, and the work is very rigid, they're probably not a good fit for their firm.) Humorous promotions are hard to pull off, which may be why many designers avoid them altogether. But when it works, as it has for the Graphik On!on, it stands out not only on its own merits, but because it's unusual.

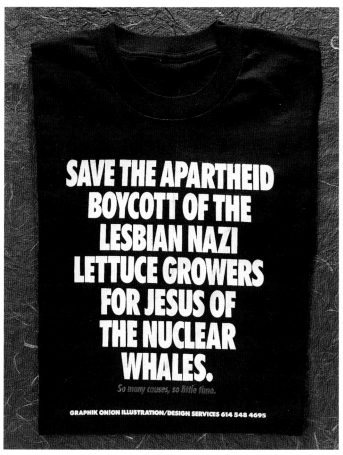

Save the . . . T-Shirt

Concept: David Cuccio, Thomas Slayton
Art Direction: David Cuccio, Thomas Slayton
Copywriting: Thomas Slayton
Quantity: 100
Budget: $389

Humor was a winning attitude for this self-promotion. The T-shirt, silkscreened in two colors, was not only popular with clients and prospects but also appeared in *Print* magazine.

Addy Ad

Concept: David Cuccio, Thomas L. Slayton
Art Direction: David Cuccio, Thomas L. Slayton
Quantity: 600 reprints
Budget: $100

To celebrate and to advertise the fact that the studio had won several Addy awards (yes, that's what those pointy objects *really* are — seen sideways), they not only ran the ad but had extras printed up for a mailing. The "shock value" and humor brought them lots of attention—and congratulatory phone calls. All retouching was done in-house.

DogStar Design Wit and Whimsy Work Wonders

After pursuing careers in both opera and graphic design for eight years, Rodney Davidson decided to concentrate on graphic design. He established DogStar Design, which specializes in logos and illustration, in Birmingham, Alabama. DogStar's work has been recognized in Print's Regional Design Annual, Step-by-Step, Graphis's Design Annual, *and* HOW. *He has also received awards from the AIGA and the National and District Addy competitions. Davidson recently came to an agreement with Terry Squire who represents him on the East Coast.*

Davidson's line work is elegant in its simplicity, but he also brings wit and whimsy to many projects—especially his self-promotion pieces. Davidson's limitless imagination is evident in his work, but he admits he has a drawer that's full of self-promotion ideas he hasn't found time to execute. When he does get around to producing a promotion piece, he gives potential clients a good idea of DogStar Design's creativity without expensive production.

Davidson's work lends itself to reproduction in black-and-white (or black on other colors), and it doesn't suffer when printed directly off his laser printer, even on construction paper. That's how his self-promotion book is produced, and this piece took Best of Show, One-Color Design, in the "Great Design in Two and Three Colors" competition run annually by Supon Phornirunlit. (It also won an award in the Curtis River Self-Promotion Contest.)

The fun Dogstar Design generates on every project is evidenced in Davidson's willingness to spin tales, including some pretty tall ones, as a running narrative about the inspiration for his work. The self-appointed "Top Dog" at DogStar describes a long and troubled relationship with dogs. While showing the "Tidbits" logo he uses on correspondence with pro bono clients, Davidson claims his first pet, Tidbit, "a saber-toothed Chihuahua," was in fact a rodent. Reality is less exciting: "tidbits" refers to the tidbits one often has to work with on pro bono jobs. (And despite that minor complaint, Davidson does a lot of pro bono work and donates his logo design services to musician friends as gifts of support.)

There may be a germ of truth in his dog stories, however. Davidson embellishes his invoices with dogs showing progressively worse tempers with each notice. He says the edgy, growling "Past Due" usually does the trick!

"Tidbits" logo

"Peacock Music Studio"—logo was donated.

"K. Lee Scott, Composer"— logo was donated.

"Past Due" — Who wouldn't pay?

Benjamin Middaugh's logo was done in trade for voice lessons. Davidson says Middaugh "truly takes his students under his wing."

Digital Prepress Services logo was done in trade for services.

DogStar Design Self-Promotion Book
Design: Rodney Davidson
Illustration: Rodney Davidson
Copywriter: Rodney Davidson
Quantity: As needed
Printed on a laser printer on an as-needed basis, usually on construction paper, the books are bound by hand. Originally put together with leftover scraps of paper, the finished product looked good enough to have been "mass produced." Davidson's rep, Terry Squire, also helps with the production of these pieces. He mails them to her flat, and she assembles them.

Peek is a Birmingham magazine established to celebrate local artists and show the diversity of talent available in the area. The premiere issue featured DogStar Design's work in the portfolio section. Davidson knew the people who started the magazine; because they were familiar with his work, they invited him to submit it for an issue.

Hodges Christmas Poster

Creative Direction: Greg Hodges
Design: Rodney Davidson
Illustration: Rodney Davidson
Copywriter: Sam Burn
Budget: Design and illustration donated

Greg Hodges, a creative director at Hodges & Associates (a local P.R. firm), asked Davidson to do this poster. Hodges had seen Davidson's work and knew of his love of music. Davidson wanted to show his work in softer colors than he usually uses, so he chose two soft colors that were close together in range—even though they weren't exactly tradition- al for Christmas.

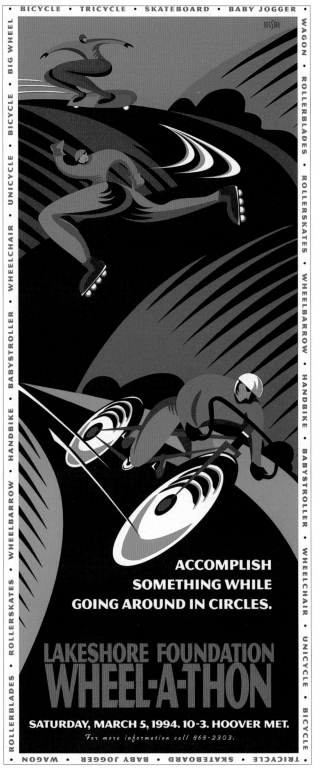

Wheel-a-Thon Poster

Design: Susan Baskin
Illustration: Rodney Davidson
Copywriter: Sam Burn
Budget: Design and illustration donated

Davidson was approached by Steiner Bressler, an advertising agency that had agreed to donate their creative services for this project. Davidson agreed to donate the illustration only if he could do it on the computer. This became his first printed piece gener- ated on the computer.

Price Elementary T-Shirt

Design: Rodney Davidson
Illustration: Rodney Davidson
Budget: Design and illustration donated
This was a pro bono project with ad agency Lewis Advertising. First Commercial Bank, one of the agency's clients, had asked them to donate creative services for this project.

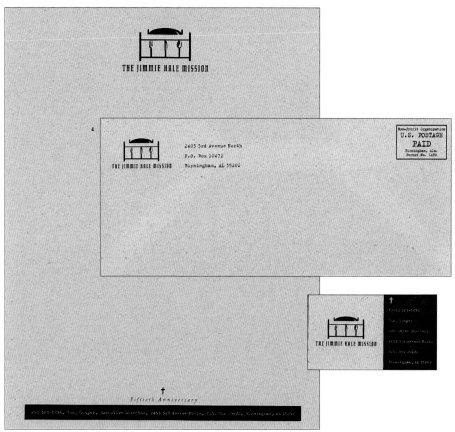

The Jimmie Hale Mission Letterhead

Art Direction: Ralph Watson
Design: Rodney Davidson
Illustration: Rodney Davidson
Budget: Design and illustration donated
The Jimmie Hale Mission was founded by Jimmie Hale, a former alcoholic who became a minister. The mission spreads the gospel and helps those in need with food, clothing and shelter. Davidson designed a letterhead that was upbeat but had an appropriately low budget. That way, Davidson says, "The recipient knows they could use the extra money."

Art Direction Getting Ahead With Humor

Chris Conerly spent twelve years working for advertising agencies, most notably, at Austin Kelly advertising agency, where he rose to creative director. Caught in a corporate downsizing two years ago, his new studio has been successful enough that he could afford to turn down a creative director position (after some agonizing) last year. He believes his studio, Art Direction, offers corporate clients agency quality and experience without the cost of agency overhead. He also continues to freelance for agencies, but he doesn't miss the politics of agency life. Conerly's work has been recognized in Print's Regional Design Annual *and* Communication Arts *and by the New York Art Directors Club.*

Chris Conerly doesn't let anything, including a limited production budget, get in the way of a good idea or a strong visual pun. That may be because production has always been his strong suit. Conerly believes he got his first agency position because he was in the right place at the right time, the art director was swamped, *and* he had production experience. While going to school full-time, he had also worked full-time doing production at a magazine company. When Conerly was an agency art director, he noticed that recent graduates of even prestigious schools seldom have production experience. He advises young designers to take a production job to get a foot in the door and as invaluable work experience.

Conerly feels that self-promotion is part of the cost of doing business as a graphic designer. If you stop swimming, you sink. He has another self-promotion idea on the table and admits that, like many other designers, he needs to promote himself "before the phone stops ringing," but it's hard to make the time for it. Conerly holds down the cost of doing promotion by relying on a strong concept and humorous presentation rather than whiz-bang production techniques.

Sometimes, less is truly more. Conerly's sly wit and knack for visual puns shines in black-and-white, eliminating the need for full-color printing. He originally shot the Van Gogh painting for his Art Direction studio identity in color, but then decided that black-and-white would be better. While brainstorming promotional ideas, a friend suggested, "It's corny, but do a notepad." Conerly knew from his agency background that the pads would be used and chose another pun for the promotional copy: "Call today for freelance creative. My pad or yours."

It's been said that timing is everything in comedy; if so, Conerly is a master. Instead of an artful verbal pause, he uses a visual one. Teaser copy on the front of a brochure or the outside of an envelope sets up the joke. Once the recipient has opened the piece, the punch line leaps out. A brochure cover is headlined, "Hire an art director who really shines..." Inside, the recipient finds a visual pun of Conerly's brightly shining bald head and the punch line, "His book isn't bad either." The envelopes that delivered his notepads to agencies and clients carried the tagline, "Finally, a promotion that's truly noteworthy."

Conerly's knack for presenting himself in a lively manner also led to some valuable, free publicity. His local suburban newspaper, the *Virginia Highlands Voice*, asked Conerly and his wife to be part of a feature on home-based businesses since they both work out of their home. He received two calls from prospective clients who had read the article. One lead fizzled out, but the other, a representative of a state and federally funded consortium, came through with a large project.

Christopher Conerly
1127 Stillwood Dr. NE
Atlanta, GA 30306

Christopher Conerly
1127 Stillwood Dr. NE
Atlanta, GA 30306
404.892.3092 fax 892.0797

Christopher Conerly
1127 Stillwood Dr. NE
Atlanta, GA 30306
404.892.3092 fax 892.0797

Art Direction Letterhead System
Art Direction: Christopher Conerly
Design: Christopher Conerly
Photography: Dave Schafer
Retouching: Danny Strickland
Quantity: 500 each
Budget: $200 to $300
A great idea doesn't need fancy production to be effective—an opinion shared in this case by *Print's Regional Design Annual* and by the New York Art Directors Club, who included this letterhead in their showcases. This visual pun is more effective in black-and-white than it would have been in color. In fact, Conerly originally had the painting shot in color but decided not to use it. One-color printing at a local quick print shop helped offset the costs of the high quality paper stock and envelopes. Conerly felt he shouldn't cut corners on the stock, because the recipients would recognize and appreciate the quality of the paper.

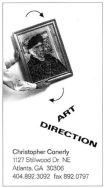

Christopher Conerly
1127 Stillwood Dr. NE
Atlanta, GA 30306
404.892.3092 fax 892.0797

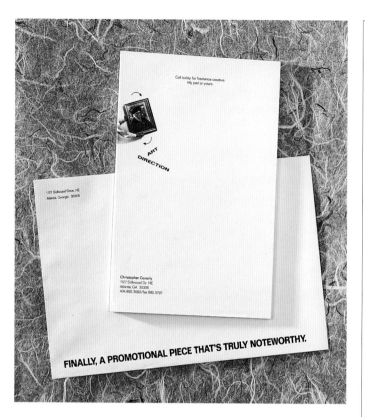

FINALLY, A PROMOTIONAL PIECE THAT'S TRULY NOTEWORTHY.

My Pad Notepad
Art Direction: Christopher Conerly
Copy: Christopher Conerly
Photography: Dave Schafer
Retouching: Danny Strickland
Quantity: 50
Budget: Approximately $100

When a friend suggested he do a notepad for a follow-up piece, Conerly knew from his own agency experience that the pads would get used. The Art Direction identity graphic on these notepads keeps his name in front of the recipients. (The pick-up of the artwork from the identity system also helped keep costs down.) The teaser copy and return address on the standard 6-1/2" x 9-1/2" envelopes was printed on a laser printer.

Who says there's no truth in advertising?

SURGEON GENERAL'S WARNING: Smoking Causes Lung Cancer, Heart Disease, Emphysema, And May Complicate Pregnancy.

AMERICAN LUNG ASSOCIATION *of Georgia*

Truth in Advertising Ad
Art Direction: Christopher Conerly
Design: Christopher Conerly
Copywriting: Christopher Conerly
Budget: Design donated

Long on message and impact, but short on production, this pro bono ad for the American Lung Association was done for a cause Conerly cares passionately about. The powerful piece has been recognized by *Communication Arts* and the New York Art Directors Club. It has also been used in a college textbook.

GIVE ME A SHINER.

I'm usually way too busy to fill out these cards, but this time I'll make an exception. Plus, you'll be sure to spell my name right.

Name_____ Title_____

Company_____

Address_____

City/State/Zip_____

Phone_____

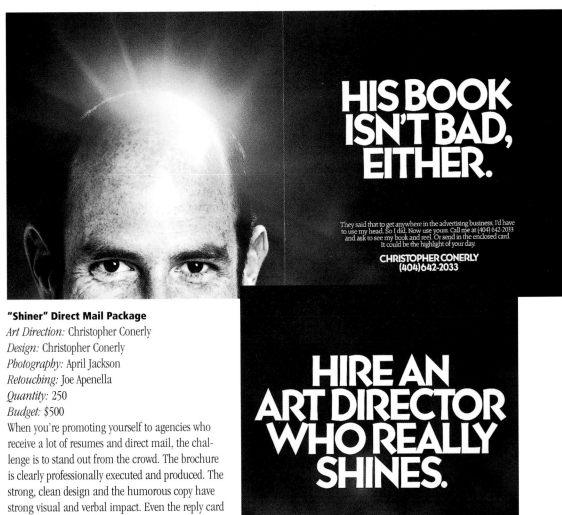

"Shiner" Direct Mail Package

Art Direction: Christopher Conerly
Design: Christopher Conerly
Photography: April Jackson
Retouching: Joe Apenella
Quantity: 250
Budget: $500

When you're promoting yourself to agencies who receive a lot of resumes and direct mail, the challenge is to stand out from the crowd. The brochure is clearly professionally executed and produced. The strong, clean design and the humorous copy have strong visual and verbal impact. Even the reply card has humorous notes, from the pun in the headline to its joking acknowledgment (based on Conerly's own agency experience) of how much mail agency art directors receive.

HIS BOOK
ISN'T BAD,
EITHER.

They said that to get anywhere in the advertising business, I'd have to use my head. So I did. Now use yours. Call me at (404) 642-2033 and ask to see my book and reel. Or send in the enclosed card. It could be the highlight of your day.

CHRISTOPHER CONERLY
(404) 642-2033

HIRE AN
ART DIRECTOR
WHO REALLY
SHINES.

THARP DID IT Keeping Tongue Firmly in Cheek

Rick Tharp studied art and advertising in the early 1970s at Miami University in Ohio. He says he liked to draw, listen to the music of the times, and drink cheap wine. Now he has his own design studio (named THARP DID IT) and four or five others doing it with him in a small town just south of San Francisco. According to Tharp, "The only thing that has really changed is the wine. It's a lot better these days."

All kinds of people from Napa Valley wineries, to Silicon Valley computer companies, to Swedish toy companies ask him to do it for them. He likes what he does and evidently so do his peers. His work is in the Smithsonian's Cooper-Hewitt Museum, and he won a Clio in 1988.

Rick Tharp keeps up a running dialogue with existing clients, friends, vendors and students through his humorous promotion efforts. He comments, verbally or visually, on whatever he finds amusing at the moment—bar codes, the design business and communication with printers, to name just a few topics. Tharp's clients are pretty hip to the design business and appreciate his sense of humor.

Tharp has a knack for putting a spin on the ordinary or obvious that makes viewers or readers sit up and take notice. He takes a similar approach to sending out his portfolio to potential clients. Each portfolio is tailored to the client, but it will often contain a few unexpected pieces that show another side of the studio. When Tharp initially approached Hewlett-Packard, he showed primarily corporate work, but he included some offbeat packaging. He was later told that the offbeat work helped him stand apart from the competition, and he now does a lot of work for Hewlett-Packard.

He does some more traditional promotion, what he calls "PR," running targeted ads in the trade publications of his clients. But after years in the design business, lots of speaking engagements at design conferences and art directors club meetings, and publication in *HOW* magazine and the design annuals, Tharp says he knows that promotion within the design industry does pay off. Other creatives and vendors enjoy and remember his promotions. They also frequently send referrals Tharp's way.

His clever takes on the UPC bar code, which he actively dislikes, have been especially well received and become a THARPish icon in the design industry. "Closely resembling stripes on a cheap suit, the typical UPC is about one inch square and consists of a series of vertical lines of various widths and spacing," is the way he puts it. The combination of lines and spaces describes the product to the retailer's scanner so it can tell the cash register how much to charge. It also tells management that the store has one less of that item in inventory. According to Tharp, "The ubiquitous UPC code is about as popular with package designers as a copyright symbol would have been to da Vinci on the Mona Lisa. We've wrestled with bar codes many times over the last twenty years, but our studio has gained a reputation for integrating the UPC code into a package's design theme on a variety of consumer package goods including wines, food and computer products. The only problem that has arisen," he laments, "is that, once in a while, the cashiers have a difficult time finding it on the package."

Tharp prefers to rely on his wit(s) rather than a computer. He says the computer is a great production tool, but a lousy design tool. He argues with his staff (who do use the computer), because he believes it gets in the way of their thinking. If it's true that the computer gets in the way of thinking and, therefore, makes for predictable solutions, then Tharp may have found yet another way to stand out in his communications by refusing to get involved with one.

Studio Promotional Cards
Design: Rick Tharp
Quantity: 6,000
Budget: $0
These cards let recipients know that the firm also does corporate identity and packaging. One of these cards is inserted into every piece of mail the studio sends out, and they're handed out with business cards. The promotional cards, which cheerfully tweak some icons of identity and design, were tagged onto the excess stock during another print run. The UPC symbol card is a reflection of the feelings most designers have toward the UPC code. Tharp presents it as a design solution rather than a problem.

GROOMING THE PRINTER

a true story

(as best can be remembered)

r i c k   t h a r p

"Grooming the Printer" Poster

Design: Rick Tharp

Quantity: 200

Budget: $200

Many friends and associates who heard Tharp's version of this story thought it was hilarious. They also thought it should be a booklet, but he thought a poster was a better medium. No typesetting was necessary; it was all produced on a Smith-Corona typewriter. A limited edition of the hand silkscreened posters was mailed...mainly to printers. That's right, printers. They all thought is was hilarious, with many asking for extras to hang in their production rooms.

Rick Tharp Biography Card

Design: Rick Tharp

Photography: Franklin Avery

Quantity: 500

Budget: $0

This card is part of a set published by Watermark Press in San Francisco. Each card features a different designer. Tharp gave his card a personal touch by banging the copy out on his typewriter, going back and restriking some letters for the rough quality. He admits it took a lot of time. The printer covered all costs on the card and gave each designer the overrun.

Bielenberg Design Making a Wry Statement

John Bielenberg is the principal of Bielenberg Design, with offices in San Francisco and Boulder, Colorado. Under his creative direction, the company has received over 150 awards from international and U.S. design organizations, including the American Institute of Graphic Arts, the American Center for Design, the Western and San Francisco Art Directors Clubs, Communication Arts, Graphis, Print, ID and Art Direction. Bielenberg's own work has been selected by the Library of Congress for its permanent Art and Design Collection. He teaches graphic design at the California College of Arts and Crafts and has been invited to judge several design competitions.

Bielenberg takes the long view toward promoting Bielenberg Design. Although his approach to promotion is a slow process, he believes that it positions him where he wants to be in the design community.

Bielenberg sees the design competition annuals as a major distribution system for self-promotion. Because his work is regularly seen in the annuals, he evaluates each of his design solutions not only for appropriateness but also with an eye to how it will be received by the design community and how it will reproduce in the small format of an annual. He sees the annuals as both blessing and burden to the design community. They are a blessing because they celebrate the high craft of graphic design. They are a burden because the pieces are presented without much, if any, sense of the piece's context. Bielenberg fears that this creates an appreciation of the surface of a design without an awareness of its real purpose: crafting a visual language that effectively communicates a message to the chosen audience.

He describes the "Warning" poster as his first direct communication to the design community. Its theme was the need for the design community to reexamine its values, goals and work. It also made a statement about waste intended to make recipients question their roles in the process of producing waste. The poster—with no commercial or promotional copy—was mailed to designers Bielenberg wanted to reach because he liked their work and what they were about professionally. Intended to be an attention-getting teaser, he didn't even include a return address. He could only produce a limited number of posters, but he knew that he could reach thousands more designers if the poster was featured in design magazines or annuals. It therefore had to be designed so it would still communicate its message when reproduced at a small size. A few designers who received the mailing were so intrigued by the poster that they traced it to its source and contacted Bielenberg. When he described an upcoming project, they loved the idea and promptly volunteered to be a part of it.

One of Bielenberg's newest projects, "The Virtual Telemetrix Annual Report," was to be a spoof on both annual reports and design competitions. The original plan was to throw a dart at a stack of annual reports and use chunks of copy from the pages he hit instead of working out "real" copy for a fictitious client. He believed that it could win an award in the annual report category—even though it was a spoof—from a committee who didn't look too closely at the content. But Bielenberg decided that was too self-serving and one-dimensional, ultimately choosing to go with a parody that pokes fun at the annual report, corporate America, and even the designer. Thoughtful designers, such as Rick Valicenti and Michael Bierut (who had discovered Bielenberg through the "Warning" poster) volunteered to contribute to the project, adding meaningful copy.

An unexpected, unintended result of the annual report spoof has been an increase in the number of annual reports Bielenberg Design gets each year. Between 1991, when the studio opened, and 1994, when the spoof appeared, the studio may have done five annual reports. In the year after the appearance of "The Virtual Telemetrix Annual Report," they worked on eight. Bielenberg remarks, "Clearly someone thought we knew a lot about annual reports." Other, more predictable, results of the promotion included invitations to speak at universities (something he enjoys doing) and an invitation to write for *Communication Arts*.

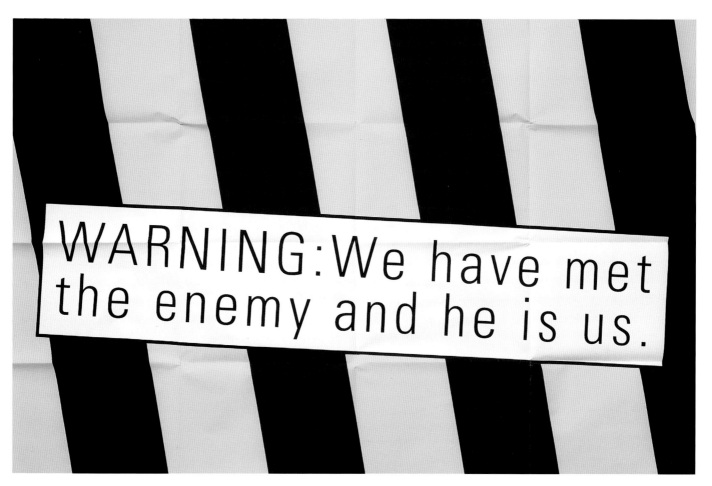

Warning Poster

Designer: John Bielenberg
Quantity: 100
Budget: $900

The poster was printed on billboard paper, folded up and mailed out with nothing on it but an address label on the envelope. (No promotional copy was included; not even a return address was used, so there was no clue as to where it came from.) The poster is much larger than it needs to be—4' x 6'—and was intended to make the design community question their role in the design/waste-generating process. Bielenberg mailed it as an attention-getting teaser to designers whose work he admired.

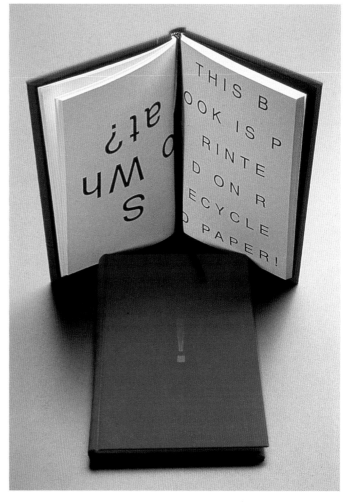

!? Book

Designers: John Bielenberg, Allen Ashton
Quantity: 40
Budget: $350

The book's copy reads, "This book is printed on recycled paper! So What?" In other words, the book has no reason to exist. This commentary on waste was sent to the design community as a follow-up to the "Warning Poster."

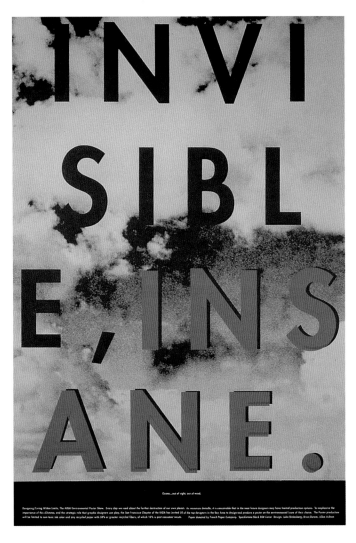

Invisible/Insane Poster

Designers: John Bielenberg, Allen Ashton,
   Brian Boram
Quantity: 50
Budget: $850

The American Institute of Graphic Arts (AIGA)
invited several designers, including Bielenberg, to
do a piece on the environment. He chose the ozone
layer as the subject for his poster and turned the
saying, "Out of sight, out of mind" into the phrase
"Invisible/Insane." The AIGA had asked for only
one original, but Bielenberg had fifty printed and
used the rest for promotion, submitting them to
design competitions and annuals.

Do You Feel Alone? Poster

Designers: John Bielenberg, Allen Ashton,
   Berndt Abeck
Quantity: 1,000
Budget: All services donated

The poster was done pro bono. The client is a nonprofit organization that helps homeless teenagers.

The Virtual Telemetrix Annual Report Spoof

Art Director: John Bielenberg
Designers: John Bielenberg, Allen Ashton,
    Brian Boram
Collaborators: Various
Quantity: 500
Budget: All services donated

Originally intended as a spoof on award contests and annual reports, the project became much more. Bielenberg had planned to illustrate the faulty thinking about design that puts appearance above content by producing a visually compelling annual report that communicated nothing. He then decided that this joke was too one-dimensional and self-serving, and the report evolved into a parody of design, annual reports and corporate America. Several designers who had received Bielenberg's series of pieces on waste contacted him about them and then volunteered to be part of this new project. These thoughtful designers contributed meaningful copy on the purpose and role of communication in the design of annual reports.

Making Special Occasions Memorable

Holidays and special occasions provide wonderful opportunities to stay in touch with clients and select prospects. Hopefully, you've developed a good relationship with your clients and want to remember them during the holidays and on special occasions.

It takes careful planning if you want to produce something special for a holiday greeting or announcement. Some of the studios in this section work months in advance and treat their holiday promotion like any other deadlined project. Holidays are the perfect time to share a message you feel is timely, or to package a gift in a unique way. Since most studios do a seasonal promotion, you'll want to make yours stand out by doing something unique, memorable and from the heart.

The **Design Company** Holiday High Note for Self-Promotion

The Design Company started in 1987 in Boston with a few small freelance accounts, limited funds and high hopes. In 1992 it became a loosely knit partnership between Marcia Romanuck and Busha Husak. After Romanuck moved to Atlanta, the partners each developed a base of clients for her office as well as projects that draw on the combined talents of the two offices. A partial list of their joint and separate clients includes the city of Atlanta, The Atlanta Downtown Partnership, the city of Boston, Cabot Corporation, the Economic Resource Group, Evan Picone, Georgia Pacific, Habersham Vineyards, the Massachusetts Bar Association, Metropolis Fine Confections, Kids II, Newport Harbor Menswear, Pure Pro Massage Oil, the Sommerset Club, South Comm Publishing and Vitamin Healthcenters.

Out of necessity, Marcia Romanuck and Busha Husak have become experts at starting up and building a design business. The original Design Company opened its doors in Boston in 1987; the second Design Company got its start in Atlanta when Marcia Romanuck moved to the sunny South and had to start the growth process all over again. Along the way their studio has grown from a small freelance studio to a successful, two-city operation, because the principals carefully targeted their marketing efforts through joint promotions focusing on clients in several industries including the food, health, clothing and consumer products industries.

Through constant referrals, leads from friends and cold calls, Romanuck and Husak have landed projects including corporate identity, packaging, collateral materials, posters, banners, publications and more. The Design Company's promotional materials are deceptive because they look as though they cost more to produce than they actually did. The studio never compromises on design but uses a variety of cost-cutting measures, such as:

- producing small quantities
- lots of handwork
- bargaining for "extras" from a client
- joining a client's print run
- shopping for bargains on materials and supplies
- taking advantage of technology

Most of the work is now computer-generated from concept through film separations. For example, cards and bottle or jar labels are sometimes run on a laser printer and visuals are more likely to be computer-generated EPS files than photographs.

Planning ahead is an important aspect of their cost-cutting efforts. Romanuck and Husak have to look at each project as an opportunity to pick up additional self-promotional materials they couldn't otherwise afford. Contracts with clients often include provisions for the Design Company to receive overruns from pieces or packaging they've designed. Romanuck and Husak approach the printer on each packaging job about the possibility of getting "fifty or so" extras from the run if they absorb any additional costs. To date, there haven't been any additional costs involved. They've also asked clients for extras for barter or at wholesale cost.

Christmas provides an important opportunity to show off the studio's package design talents with seasonal promotions to potential and existing clients in the food and retail industry. Romanuck and Husak have considered doing their promotion at a different time of the year, but with other studios sending gifts and promos at Christmas, they feel they should, too. The Christmas promotion is their major effort each year; the rest of the year they seek referrals and send the occasional postcard to stay in touch with existing clients.

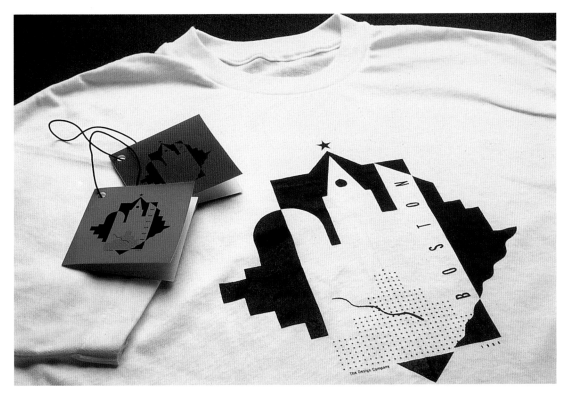

The Design Company T-Shirt

Design: Marcia Romanuck, Denise Pickering
Quantity: 36
Budget: $200
White T-shirts were silkscreened with black ink and given as Christmas presents. The gift cards create the holiday tie-in. The cards were produced by running red and green Kromekote through a copy machine.

Holiday Wine

Design: Marcia Romanuck, Busha Husak
Quantity: 100
Budget: $300
The label art was generated on the computer and output as color laser proofs on a Canon Fiery printer. To give the labels a slicker look, and to intensify the colors, the sheets were laminated. The labels were then cut by hand and spray mounted on the bottles. The Design Company bartered with a client for the bottles of wine.

Nancy Doniger Illustration New Year's "Memora-Mobilia"

Nancy Doniger of Nancy Doniger Illustration in Brooklyn studied at the Art Students League, Parson, the SVA, and the New York Studio School of Painting and Sculpture. Her media is cut rubylith, cut paper and/or computer. Her clients include the New York Times, *the* Wall Street Journal, *AT&T, Citibank, HarperCollins and Macmillan.*

People remember the mobiles that Nancy Doniger sends as New Year's promotions; some clients even display them in their homes or offices all year. Because of the time required to do the cutting and the assembly, Doniger limits the quantity to one hundred each year. She sends the mobiles to clients to thank them and to important prospective clients to

entice them to offer her work. Many clients have the whole set and look forward to the new mobile each year. Doniger believes, "They make people smile, and that helps my relationship with them."

Doniger says her major inspirations for the mobiles are a feeling of "joy," a love of movement, and her son, Cody. All the pieces of each mobile are black and white, and the designs always include pictures of Cody (although some people may not have noticed). As Cody has grown, so have the children in the illustrations for the mobiles.

The movement in Doniger's mobiles is achieved with string and paper clips. Each is mailed or delivered by hand inside a piece of card-

board that protects the fragile pieces.

Doniger's friend Beata Szpura, also an illustrator, helps Doniger get motivated for the major task of putting the mobiles together. Because Szpura also does mobiles that require a lot of handwork each year, the two women get each other psyched for the task and "compete" in a friendly way.

Doniger reinforces her holiday promos with another black-and-white promo — this one a pro bono piece. She designed a set of note cards with illustrations of children printed in black ink on white card stock. She uses the cards herself, but they are also sold, with the proceeds helping to support Brooklyn Free Space, a cooperative preschool.

Nancy Doniger Blank Note Cards
Design: Nancy Doniger
Illustration: Nancy Doniger
Budget: Design donated
These strong illustrations don't need four-color printing to make an impact. Sales of the popular note cards benefit the Brooklyn Free Space, a cooperative preschool, and Doniger uses some herself as a promotional tool.

Nancy Doniger New Year's Promos

Design: Nancy Doniger
Illustration: Nancy Doniger
Production: Nancy Doniger
Quantity: 100 each year
Budget: $20 to $30

Nancy photocopies her black-and-white illustrations onto white letter-size card stock. She then cuts and assembles each mobile by hand with paper clips and string. A hand-written note on the back personalizes each mobile, and they are sent only to special clients and important prospects.

Mark Oldach Design Sending a Message From the Heart

Mark Oldach received his design training at Carnegie-Mellon University and then held positions with several not-for-profit and socially conscious organizations in Washington, D.C. He returned to the Midwest and worked at several design firms before heading the creative department for the American Medical Association. Mark founded his own design firm, Mark Oldach Design, in 1989; his varied client base includes both not-for-profit and for-profit organizations. He has been honored, exhibited and published nationally, including the ACD 100 Show and the Type Directors Club. His firm's work has appeared in such noted publications as Communication Arts, ID Magazine, AIGA Communication Graphics, Graphis, Print *and* HOW *and has been recognized by numerous paper companies, including Gilbert Paper and Neenah Paper. In 1995, Mark published a book exploring the creative process from initial client contact to the creative conclusion,* Creativity for Graphic Designers *(North Light Books). His list of accomplishments also includes speaking and judging engagements. He is a member of the American Institute of Graphic Arts and the American Center for Design.*

Mark Oldach Design's clients look forward to the studio's annual Christmas card. They even call to make sure they're still on the mailing list.

The holiday project is the primary promotional effort for the studio each year. They begin work in September and devote a solid three months of work to it around and between projects for clients. Oldach and his staff find that having a solid, unbreakable deadline forces them to focus on the self-promotion, treating the studio as if it were a client. (One year, other obligations did require them to change the deadline from Christmas to New Year's Eve, but it didn't slip any further.)

Oldach tries to do in his own promotion what he does for clients, with an execution consistent with the concept. Each piece begins with conceptual work with a writer, because he wants clients and potential clients to "see how we think." Those who do respond turn out to be a good match for the studio, appreciating the amount of thought and care the studio puts into all its work.

The words chosen for a piece are very important in the work Oldach does both for his clients and for himself. The message, often personal and always warmly emotional, is precious. The message winds through the cards, which are more like books, and even the line breaks in the copy play an important role. Oldach forces his clients, who tend to be verbally and visually sophisticated, to think as he strikes an emotional chord. He feels that you will be remembered if you appeal honestly to the emotions of your audience. It has certainly been true for him. One prospect was so

moved by his "Family" self-promotion booklet (facing page) that she kept it on her desk for six months, waiting to call Oldach for just the right project. That perfect project never materialized, but a huge design program did. She is now the studio's biggest client.

Although Oldach's promotions are never overproduced, and many have been inexpensive, he insists that you have to pay for a certain production quality or value. "Dirty Secrets" (see page 81) was done within a set, rather tight, budget, and Oldach feels it shows. He also points out that it's easier to attract clients who'll pay for more color on their jobs if you use more than two colors on your own promotions. Part of the three months' work on the holiday promotion is budgeted for hand assembly and other handwork; this helps offset the costs of other aspects of production. The most grueling piece the studio ever tackled was "The Circle Widens" (page 80). Hand assembling each one saved roughly $700 on binding, and there were personal rewards as well. Many clients and friends incorporated the promotion into their Christmas celebrations and shared their stories with the studio afterward.

Oldach's insistence on quality production has also affected his work for pro bono clients, such as local arts organizations. He has stopped finding printers who will donate their services for such projects. If he buys services at fair value, Oldach can complain if quality standards aren't met instead of being obligated to accept what's given as a donation. He also feels that the credit line received for pro bono work seldom fully compensates the separators and printers who donate their services.

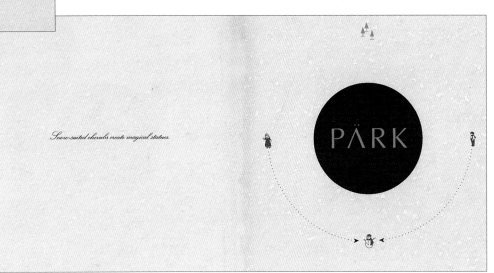

Hark Christmas Card
Concept: Mark Oldach
Design: Mark Oldach
Copywriting: Linda Chryle
Quantity: 700
Budget: $2,500
Oldach did this Christmas card his first year in business. Words that rhyme with "hark" weave a playful message throughout. The final page is "Seasons Greetings" from "Mark."

Family Christmas Card/Booklet
Concept: Mark Oldach
Design: Mark Oldach
Copywriting: Linda Chryle, Mark Oldach
Photography: Kechele and Oldach families
Quantity: 700
Budget: $7,000
This Christmas card is a celebration of family, typical of the emotional nature of Oldach's work. It received a tremendous response from clients, friends and fellow designers, and was directly responsible for attracting his biggest client.

Katy Rose Oldach Birth Announcement
Concept: Mark Oldach
Design: Mark Oldach
Copywriting: Mark Oldach and Linda Chryle
Photography: Anthony Arciero
Quantity: 1,000
Budget: $3,500
Oldach did the announcement as something personal primarily for friends and family. But since he tends to be close to his clients, they too were aware of the pregnancy. The photos and the smooth-textured paper and binding are reminiscent of babies and baby things. Some of the announcements were fastened with a diaper pin.

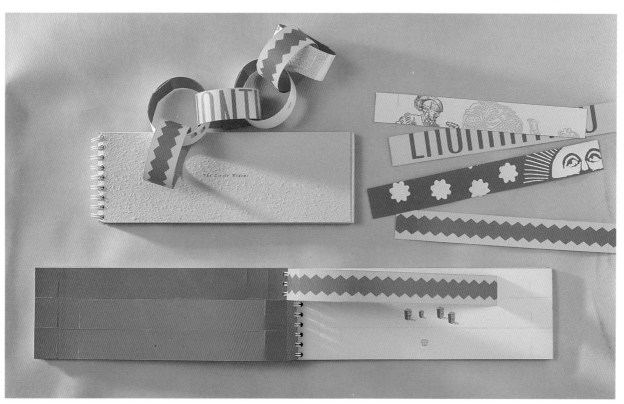

The Circle Widens Book/Ornament
Concept: Mark Oldach
Design: Don Emery and Mark Oldach
Copywriting: Linda Chryle
Quantity: 700
Budget: $5,000
This book/ornament was hand-bound by Oldach and his staff. He still describes it as a "painful process," but the studio had the time, making it cost-effective. (It would not have been cost-effective if time were taken away from other jobs, in which case they would have chosen another option.) There was a lot of die-cutting in the piece, but the binding would have cost an additional dollar per piece if some of it were not done by hand.

Dirty Secrets Promotion

Concept: Mark Oldach
Design: Mark Oldach
Copywriting: Mark Oldach
Quantity: 200
Budget: $1,000
This was originally done as a presentation. When the project didn't materialize, Oldach decided to recoup some of the time he had invested in the presentation by producing it as a promotional piece. Inexpensive charms attached to the piece by a short, self-locking chain add a note of intrigue that perfectly suits the title.

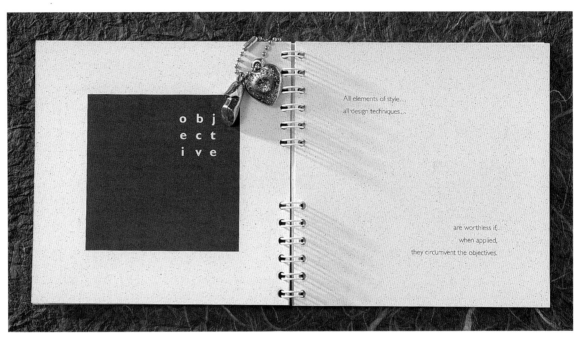

Midnight Book

Concept: Mark Oldach
Design: Mark Oldach
Copywriting: Linda Chryle
Photography: Anthony Arciero
Quantity: 1,000
Budget: $5,000
The black-and-white photos add a surreal quality to this one-color piece. Die-cut circles on each panel reveal the clock image peering out through every right-hand page; looking back at the left hand page, viewers find a flower has appeared in place of the clock.

Tin Box Studio Making Occasions Special

Sandy Weinstein started Tin Box Studio in 1993 after seven years as a corporate art director and a total of fifteen years as an art director and designer. She served as president of the Art Directors Club of Cincinnati for two consecutive terms and has been on the organization's executive board since 1987 in various positions. She's successfully completed book covers, packaging design, letterhead, magazine and newspaper advertising, and corporate identities. Her clients include her former employer, South-Western Publishing Co., and Provident Bank. She also designs miniatures and is currently building a dollhouse.

Sandy Weinstein wasted no time getting on her feet after she was politely shown the door during a round of corporate downsizing. (The copy on her first mailer announcing the move illustrates her positive approach with a cheerful reference to the change: "When I left South-Western, I just kept heading south-west.") Weinstein promoted her new studio through local contacts and net-working skills developed during years of serving the Cincinnati design com-munity in various positions in local design organizations. She also had a long list of contacts and potential referrals outside the city that she had developed while contracting work for her former employer and through her roles with the Art Directors Club of Cincinnati, where she met nationally recognized designers, photographers and illustrators. Weinstein's ability to adapt quickly to her changed circum-stances brought her not only work but coverage in the design press as well. *HOW* magazine profiled her for the *1995 Business Annual*, an event she celebrated by sending one hun-dred overruns of the article to poten-tial clients.

Weinstein describes her work as "bright" and "high energy." She shows the kind of work she wants to get in her portfolio. She says the look trans-lates well for a variety of clients, even a bank. One client told her that they'd seen a lot of books, but they wanted to see more of hers because most of the other work they had seen was so

dark. Weinstein has always favored bright colors, an attitude reflected in her choice of a splash of bright yel-low to accent her new studio's logo and letterhead system. The variety of cards in the system also demonstrates her organizational skills. Virtually every inch on the printer's sheet was used for address labels, business cards, note cards, disk labels, hang tags and thank-you note cards.

After sharing space with another designer for one and a half years, Weinstein celebrated her business suc-cess by moving to a new space. Her announcement was a bright, cheerful collage of flowers, fruit, vegetables and birds, typical of her fun, eclectic design style, that she "printed" on a color photocopier. About that time, a paper rep who had known Weinstein for years called on her with some bright hued papers and said, "I just knew you'd love these." The rep was right; Weinstein used them to announce the open house she held after moving her studio to its second location. (See page 84.) Her first two holiday promotions are as cheerful and colorful as her other pieces. One year she sent M&M candies (how much more colorful can you get?) in a tin with hangtags and ribbons in her "signature yellow." A small house-shaped tin box filled with a bag of cookies was decorated by a brightly colored card in vivid red, green, blue, purple and, of course, the signature yellow.

Tin Box Studio Letterhead System

Art Direction: Sandy Weinstein
Design: Sandy Weinstein
Quantity: 500
Budget: $685

Weinstein's letterhead system is silent testimony to what can be done with good organization: her return address labels, note cards, hang tags, disk labels and thank you cards are all included, and virtually every spot on the printer's sheet was used. She scanned her letterhead paper to get the background on the mailing labels. Weinstein also had stickers that "could be used on anything" printed. When she moved to new space, she reprinted her letterhead, but had the old letterhead cut down—cutting off the old address—and used it for note pads.

Weinstein purchased one hundred overruns of the article featuring her studio in the *1995 HOW Business Annual*, put them in sleeves with her label, and mailed them to potential clients. She also mailed a press release on her stationery.

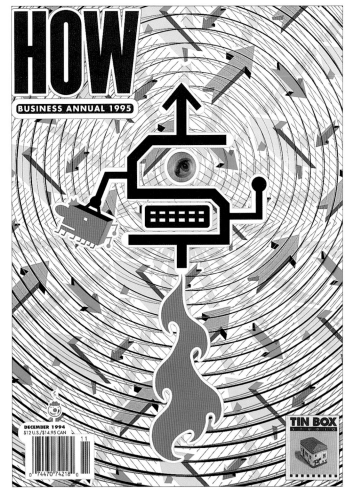

Tin Box Studio Moving Announcement

Design: Sandy Weinstein
Illustration: Sandy Weinstein
Quantity: 200
Budget: $142 ($78 plus $64 postage)

Weinstein combined the original art for this card with a collection of stickers from the 1950s and 1960s that she had found at a garage sale. She added handwritten and laser output text for the messages. The announcements were laid out two-up, and color photocopied on card stock, by hand.

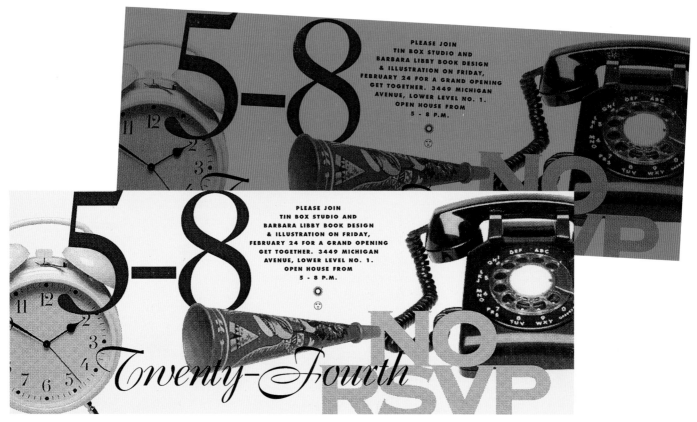

Tin Box Studio Open House Invitation

Art Direction: Sandy Weinstein
Design: Sandy Weinstein
Quantity: 200
Budget: $99 (for the illustrations; $0 to print)

Weinstein got extra Hammermill Brite Hue paper samples from her rep. She used images from the Image Club "Object Gear" CD for the illustrations. The invitations were printed two-up from her laser printer and trimmed out by hand.

Tin Box Studio Holiday Promo (Candy)

Art Direction: Sandy Weinstein

Design: Sandy Weinstein

Quantity: 72

Budget: $200 (tins, candy and postage)

Weinstein bought the tins, which she personalized with her pre-printed hangtags and some cards, to hold M&M candies. She added ribbon in her "signature yellow."

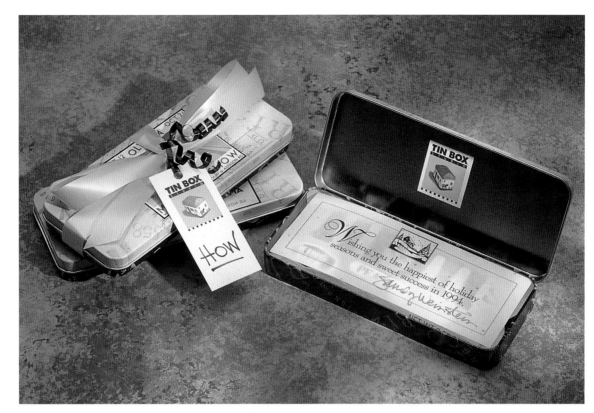

Tin Box Studio Holiday Promo (Cookies)

Art Direction: Sandy Weinstein

Design: Sandy Weinstein

Quantity: 30

Budget: $300 (cookies, tins, cards and postage)

Weinstein found these colorful tins and decided they would be perfect for her next Christmas promotion. She filled each tin with a bag of Famous Amos cookies, wishing her clients Season's Greetings "from Sandy and Amos." The cards were output from Weinstein's printer and color photocopied.

Phoenix Creative Hot Theme for Holiday Promotions

Phoenix Creative is a thirty-person multi-disciplinary design firm located in St. Louis. Working in corporate identity, packaging, sales promotion and corporate communications, the staff continually learns from the entire spectrum of design problem-solving. "You never know from one week to the next what mix of projects we'll be tackling," says Eric Thoelke, Phoenix's creative director. "One week we're designing a sophisticated corporate identity program for an international software developer, and the next we're creating a wild-and-crazy sales promotion display that's going to be in every Walgreens from Maine to Walla Walla. It all keeps us fresh." In 1994, Phoenix Creative won over fifty local and national design awards for clients ranging from Anheuser-Busch and Compaq Computer to a small, local art-furniture store. "Variety is everything here," says Thoelke. "When we start to get bored, we're dead."

One of the challenges for a studio that works for such a diverse range of clients is creating self-promotion that walks a knife-edge between being conservative enough for its corporate design clients yet exciting enough for its sales promotion clients. "We don't want anyone thinking we're the 'wrong kind' of firm to work with them," says Ed Mantels-Seeker, one of Phoenix's senior designers, "so the solutions we come up with have to be playful, but sophisticated. It's a small target to hit." Just to make things harder, Phoenix has linked all of its self-promotions with the theme "St. Louis' Hottest Creative Comes From Phoenix." Mantels-Seeker explains, "On everything from our letterhead to the hot, buttered popcorn we send to prospective clients, every time we communicate with our clients we are selling the message that we are the place to go for hot ideas." To that end, the company's client gifts in 1993 and 1994 both used "hot" themes.

Phoenix is also unique among St. Louis design firms in having both in-house full-time illustrators and in-house color laser and black-and-white repro imaging equipment. "By keeping tight control over the creative process at every step, we are able to produce a better product faster—and often less expensively—than our competition," says Steve Spingmeyer, Phoenix's President. Phoenix illustrators executed final airbrush artwork, and the computer production staff created final trapped-and-separated film negatives for the printer on their intricate "Chili Pepper Lights" gift box (page 88). The "Hot Times Clocks" promotion (page 89) was designed and illustrated completely on Phoenix's Macintosh computers, then output directly in color on their Silicon Graphics Cyclone/Canon copier system. This in-house capability allowed them to cost-effectively create six clock versions to allow for almost *individual* targeting of their clients. There are both male- and female-faced clocks, each available in three different copy versions: "Under the Gun," "Getting the Message" and "Getting the Point." "The trick to these self-promotions," says Springmeyer, "is doing something that looks like a million, but isn't really a budget-buster."

1992 Holiday Party Invitation and The Forgotten Forest Gift Package

Creative Direction: Eric Thoelke

Design: Eric Thoelke (book), Ed Mantels-Seeker (packaging and invitation)

Copywriting: Judy Milanovitz (invitation)

Photography: Michael Eastman

Computer production: Kathy Christoferson

Quantity: 150 of each

Budget: $800 (printing and die-cutting)

    Invitation per unit cost: $2.13

    Gift package per unit cost: $3.23

The invitation and gift enclosure sheet were run in conjunction with a client's holiday promotion, providing substantial savings on the five-match-color printing. Film negatives were provided by Phoenix via their in-house imagesetting. The wrappers for the invitation and gift book were sized to efficiently die-cut out of the same sheet and were left unprinted to contain costs. Copies of the eighty-page book Phoenix designed (for the photographer's own self-promotion) were provided at no cost. The assembly of both pieces was done in-house. Most of the gift packages were delivered by Phoenix's sales staff, avoiding additional protective packaging and courier or mailing costs.

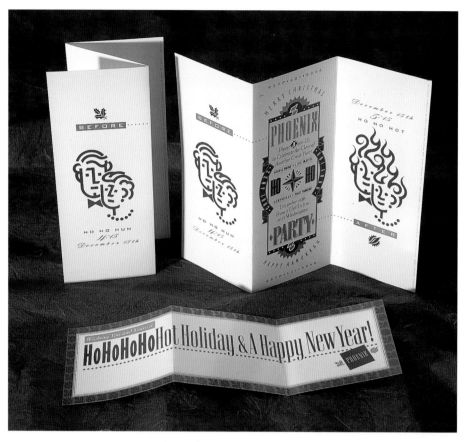

1993 Holiday Party Invitation and Chili Pepper Lights Gift Package

Creative Direction: Eric Thoelke

Art Direction: Ed Mantels-Seeker

Design: Ed Mantels-Seeker

Copywriting: Ed Mantels-Seeker

Illustration: Ed Mantels-Seeker (invitation), Mike Neville (gift package)

Computer production: Terry Laupp

Quantity: 150 of each

Budget: $2,140

    Invitation per unit cost: $2.00

    Gift package per unit cost: $12.26

The invitation, gift box wrapper, and enclosure card were piggy-backed on a client's holiday promotion. Run with this six-match-color job, it was then passed back through the press for four-color process (on the packaging's full-color spot illustrations) and a gloss aqueous coating. Phoenix accurately produced pre-trapped film negatives on the match-color part of the job to further reduce printing costs. As a result, a lavish ten-color job (including some metallic inks) was produced for the much lower cost of four-color printing.

1994 Holiday Party Invitation and Hot Times Clock Gift Package

Creative Direction: Eric Thoelke

Design: Ed Mantels-Seeker (invitation and gift package), Eric Thoelke (gift package)

Copywriting: Ed Mantels-Seeker, Eric Thoelke, Steve Springmeyer

Illustration: Ed Mantels-Seeker

Computer production: Ann Guillot

Quantity: 200 of each

Budget: $2,860

Invitation per unit cost: $1.00

Gift package per unit cost: $13.30

The invitation was economically "ganged" with a client's six-match-color, eight-up business card form and then passed back through the press for the two-match-color side. The gift box was screen printed in two match colors on both sides and then finished using several "labels" gang printed on Phoenix's in-house color copier. The clocks were purchased at wholesale directly from the manufacturer. All gluing and assembly of the boxes and clock faces was done in-house. The result was Phoenix's most visually rich promotion yet, one that would have been unaffordable if produced otherwise.

Vaughn Wedeen Creative Becoming More Than a Local Studio

Steve Wedeen and Rick Vaughn met in Albuquerque, where they started sharing space with two other designers. They had a different vision from the others in the loosely affiliated "Design Group," so they started Vaughn Wedeen Creative in 1982. Four years later, Richard Kuhn joined the studio as account manager and copywriter, becoming a partner in 1989. Over half their clients—which include Lasertechnics, Taos Furniture, the University of New Mexico, Jones Intercable, US West, the Santa Fe Opera, Levi Strauss & Co., Beckett Paper and Gilbert paper— are based outside New Mexico. Along the way, they've picked up hundreds of awards and recognition in a variety of design publications.

In a little over ten years, Vaughn Wedeen Creative has grown from a little-known studio in a small city to a regional powerhouse that draws over half its clients from outside New Mexico. This unlikely success story is even more remarkable since it began far from the major design centers in a community that had quite a few advertising agencies and no design studios when Steve Wedeen and Rick Vaughn first reached Albuquerque. (In fact, the fledgling studio was met with some hostility at first, because they refused to do the spec work typical of the advertising industry.)

Part of their success story is being able to supply many of their own production services. This means that Vaughn, Wedeen and their third partner, Richard Kuhn, can live where they want yet still work easily and efficiently with clients across the country.

But the true secret of their success is outstanding design combined with the salesmanship of Richard Kuhn. Although Kuhn's primary responsibility is bringing in work, all three partners work at persuading clients of the benefits of working with Vaughn Wedeen Creative. Wedeen observes, "In some way, every project we do is self-promotion." Of course, any design has to get results for the client, but the whole body of Vaughn Wedeen's work also gets results for the studio. Kuhn travels and shows the studio's portfolio, often elevating a client's standards for design and expanding the studio's role in a project. He enjoys the challenge of educating corporate clients who love the studio's work but worry about the effect of going beyond the expected on their own projects. One way the studio gets the freedom they need to

do such high-quality work is to put the audience first, reminding nervous clients that they—and their customers—appreciate communication that is interesting to look at and aesthetically appealing. Many clients, from local retail stores to Fortune 500 giants, have been convinced to take risks, take chances. They deserve credit, too, for having the courage to innovate.

When Vaughn and Wedeen first started their studio, they did a lot of local pro bono work—and still do. (Vaughn's work has always had a Southwestern flavor, but Wedeen likes to be a little more cosmopolitan.) They felt that promoting Albuquerque as a sophisticated city would help the city—and generate more clients for the studio down the road. Vaughn Wedeen takes on only the projects they feel deserve the quality design the studio can bring to the work. Among the studio's best known pro bono projects are the "Zoo Boo" posters for an annual fund-raiser in memory of the sister of one of Steve Wedeen's friends.

Vaughn and Wedeen try to create work for their clients, and especially their own promotions, that people don't want to throw away, pieces that are "artifacts." Wedeen argues that you don't necessarily have to spend a fortune to create something truly valuable. Many of the studio's holiday promotions have featured handmade, edible goodies. Clients receive the inexpensively produced packages with glee, and the studio enjoys the opportunity to show off its packaging skills. In keeping with their hometown emphasis, many of the gift foodstuffs have a strong Southwestern flavor.

Holiday Treats Christmas Promotion

Art Direction: Rick Vaughn
Design: Rick Vaughn, Nicky Ovitt
Illustration: Nicky Ovitt
Mechanical production: Vivian Harder
Computer production: Nicky Ovitt
Hand Lettering: Nicky Ovitt
Quantity: 350
Budget: Under $1,200
This Christmas promotion was baked, hand assembled and mailed by Vaughn Wedeen employees. A recipe book containing recipes from the staff is enclosed with each gift. More than a gift from the Southwest, this promotion was a gift from the kitchens of the studio.

Vinegar & Chutneys Christmas Promotion

Art Direction: Daniel Flynn, Steve Wedeen, Rick Vaughn
Design: Daniel Flynn
Illustration: Bill Gerhold
Mechanical production: Nanci Easter
Computer production: Nathan James
Vinegar & chutneys: Helen Harriet Bouck
Quantity: 350
Budget: Approximately $40 each
In addition to making a rich, colorful package, the delicious vinegar and chutneys are homemade by a local Albuquerque woman in her nineties. The unusual gifts were well-received by clients and friends. Both offset printing and silkscreening were used on this promotion.

Gizmo Christmas Promotion

Art Direction: Rick Vaughn
Design: Rick Vaughn
Photography: David Nufer
Quantity: 200
Budget: Varied

After several years of Christmas promotions with food gifts, Vaughn Wedeen wanted to do something different. Each staff member had three weeks to make a toy from a canister of brightly colored wood and metal parts. They were then photographed with their toys. For the actual promotion, the studio mailed out these photos with a canister of the parts. Recipients were then asked to send in photos of themselves with the toys *they* created. More than a break with their own holiday tradition, this promotion gave the studio an opportunity to let clients see them as individuals.

1993 Aids Walk Poster

Art Direction: Rick Vaughn
Design: Lisa Graff
Illustration: Lisa Graff
Quantity: 5,500
Budget: All services donated

Vaughn and Wedeen are willing to hustle for donated services and materials because they believe in the causes they help promote. The partners feel that quality graphics, posters and T-shirts give legitimacy to an event and elevate its status in the community. They draw on their own connections to make sure an event has the quality graphics it deserves.

The 1993-94 Manzano Day School Calendar

Art Direction: Steve Wedeen

Design: Steve Wedeen

Illustration: Stan McCoy, Vivian Harder

Copywriter: Nathan James

Mechanical Production: Vivian Harder, Stan McCoy

Quantity: 1,000

Budget: Design services donated

This calendar, designed for his daughter's school, illustrates Wedeen's approach to pro bono work. Wedeen knew that the school, parents and children deserved something better than the 8-1/2" x 11" calendar with fractional black-and-white ads that the school had asked him to design. He came up with the idea of selling sponsorships. Sponsors would submit trivia about their businesses to be used on the calendars instead of running ads. Wedeen convinced the school to try the sponsorships, and the resulting calendar (now an annual project) has been a big success.

Zoo Boo 3 Poster

Art Direction: Steve Wedeen

Design: Steve Wedeen

Illustration: Steve Wedeen

Quantity: 500

Budget: All services donated

This is the third in a series of posters done pro bono for an annual zoo event. The event is held in the memory of Shelly Lerner Bernstein, a volunteer at the zoo and the sister of one of Wedeen's friends. The first year, a former client of Vaughn Wedeen's agreed to sponsor the event — but specifically requested that Vaughn Weeden do the graphics for it.

Winner Koenig Celebrations

Winner Koenig & Associates is an eighteen-person, Tampa agency. With their dual emphasis on doing and promoting both advertising and design, they have had some very comprehensive projects. One project, the redesign of the graphic identity of a chain of grocery stores in Florida, included environmental graphic design for the interior and exterior of the stores, as well as design of uniforms, store-brand labels, grocery bags and more. The work for the U-Save Supermarkets also encompassed an award-winning advertising campaign, including color newspaper ads, TV spots and outdoor advertising. Current projects include advertising and design for Joffrey's Coffee Co., a rapidly growing chain of gourmet coffee shops. This design work will introduce a new image carried through in packaging, signage, posters, gift items, uniforms and interior design. At the same time, a series of small, humorous newspaper ads will be running.

Basically, the creative team's philosophy is that every aspect of their work should be well-designed, including the advertising. Two of their recent campaigns, one for a hospital, another for a university, incorporated type from the print work into some beautifully designed television spots.

Being a relatively small agency, Winner Koenig often has to work with limited budgets for their clients. What better way to demonstrate the ability to do this without compromising integrity and creativity, than through their own self-promotions?

Some people know how to make any occasion a celebration. That's definitely true of the staff at Winner Koenig & Associates in Tampa. They see promotions for special occasions and holidays as an opportunity to express the staff's creativity. Although the results are well-designed and quite sophisticated, the pieces still express a childlike sense of fun and excitement.

Their special occasion promotions are not merely creative self-expression, they're also carefully planned to appeal to and involve the audience. The campaign for the Creative Club of Tampa Bay (page 96) is a good example of their approach. Since creative people often feel "oppressed" by clients, lack of opportunity and bills (just to name a few sore points), the theme of "Creative Revolution" was chosen for the campaign. The audience responded enthusiastically to the invitation to attend a "Working Class Party." Arm bands were distributed at the party, and those who joined became "Card-Carrying Members" of the club.

The holiday promotion, "Seasons Greetings From Olive Us at Winner Koenig" shows just how far you can take an illustration. Four different labels were designed and illustrated—a toy soldier, a snowman, a reindeer and a Santa Claus — all constructed from olives and toothpicks. These were then wrapped around jars of olives and given as presents. Each

package also included a booklet offering recipes for olives, as well as more ways to illustrate with one.

The agency again targeted both current and prospective clients, as well as friends, with a special self-promotion for its fifth anniversary. The copy ties together the theme of the piece, the meaning of "five," and relates it to the client's own interest, getting good work. Joni Spencer says, "The way the concept came together actually served to explain our philosophy of creating a piece by looking at each project in a new way—of taking the expected and creating something unexpected."

The fifth anniversary project also illustrates the agency's group approach to producing a great self-promotion without having an extravagant budget. Since they were celebrating the agency's anniversary, everyone was asked to contribute their ideas of the meaning of "five." Many of those ideas were woven into the piece. Production was also a group effort. The staff cut windows by hand, bound the booklets, and stuffed and addressed them for mailing. Everyone also pitched in on the "Olive Greeting," removing old labels, applying new ones, folding the inserts and packaging the gifts for mailing.

Fifth Anniversary Brochure

Creative Direction: Joni Spencer
Design: Julie Davis
Copywriting: Joni Spencer
Photographer: Gary Resnick
Quantity: 700
Budget: $4,000

Winner Koenig wanted to visually intrigue and involve the recipients of this fifth anniversary brochure with images and words that mean "five," such as a family of five, a five-pointed star, the fifth amendment, the five senses, etc. They even used traditional fifth anniversary gifts to make the piece: wood (the stick) and paper. The cover is Twin Rocker Heartland hand-made paper, and the brochure is packaged in a sturdy paper sealed with a sticker closure for mailing. The piece is printed in three colors with duotones and tri-tones on a single side of the sheet. The window in the front cover was hand-cut by the Winner Koenig staff, who also bound the booklets and wrapped them for mailing.

Olive Greeting Holiday Promotion

Design: Julie Davis
Illustration: Julie Davis
Copywriter: Joni Spencer
Quantity: 650
Budget: $3,000

"Season's Greetings From Olive Us at Winner Koenig" is the cheerful message of this holiday promotion. Each bottle was packaged with a booklet entitled "Entertaining With Olives," inspired by old 1950s cookbooks that always included exciting tips for entertaining. Although olive green and dark red aren't typical holiday colors, they still fit into the seasonal picture. Both the booklet and the labels were printed in three match colors on one side of tan Fox River Confetti 100-pound text. All pieces were gang printed on the same sheet of paper.

Creative Club of Tampa Bay Membership Campaign

Design: Julie Davis
Illustrator: Phillip Bennett
Copywriter: Joni Spencer
Slogan: Gordon Myhre
Quantity: 1,500
Budget: $1,900 (some services donated)

This campaign for the Creative Club of Tampa Bay urged advertising and design creatives to "Unite" and join the "Creative Revolution." It included a poster and an invitation to attend a membership party billed as a "Working Class Party." The slogan, "Men and Women in Advertising Unite" was coined by photographer Gordon Myhre and inspired the choice of Russian constructivist style design that carried the theme forward. The copy also follows the theme with references to the "Creative Manifesto" and the need to "rise above the masses" and find the creative revolution within. All who joined received cards identifying them as "Card Carrying Members" of the club.

Samata Associates Great Things Come in Small Packages

Pat and Greg Samata are partners in life and in Samata Associates, their Dundee, Illinois, studio. They focus on corporate identity, and financial and corporate communications for a select group of clients, including Georgia-Pacific, Helene Curtis and the Upjohn Co. Their award-winning work has appeared in many publications and shows, including Print, *the Mead Annual Report Show, the 100 Show, and* Graphis Annual Reports. *Pat Samata was named 1990-91 Woman of the Year by Women in Design. Greg Samata was recently a member of the AIGA national board of directors. Both judge and lecture extensively throughout the United States.*

The Samatas wanted to announce the birth of their son, Parker. He was a premature baby, weighing under four pounds at birth, inspiring the theme, "Great Things Come in Small Packages." The piece was mailed to friends, family and clients, who responded with lots of smiles and baby gifts.

The black pages and accordion fold suggest old family photograph albums. An actual photo of Parker has been glued to one page. The front and back cover are embellished with baby's hand and footprint, with a white-on-white look that makes them appear to be part of the fabric of the cover material itself.

Parker Hart Samata Birth Announcement
Design: Pat and Greg Samata
Photography: Marc Norberg
Printing: Great Northern Printing
Quantity: 500
Budget: All services donated

The photographer and printer both donated their services for the occasion. The papers — Champion Carnival, White Groove and Black Vellum — were contributed by Champion Paper. The booklet unfolds into something much bigger than it appears to be at first; a very appropriate thing for a birth announcement.

Benefiting by and From Pro Bono

The ideal pro bono project gives you an opportunity to support a cause you believe in and do the kind of work you want to do. If you're just starting out, pro bono work may be your best printed work and can help you establish credibility. When you and your client are a good fit, both parties benefit.

Since your credit line and some printed pieces are your payment, you should choose your causes carefully and make sure that the exposure you get compensates you for your investment of time and talent. The studios in this section have achieved mutually beneficial arrangements that promote their client's goals while showcasing their talents.

Artworks Helping Others Grow

Vicki Rice started Artworks in Indianapolis, Indiana, with her friend Marilyn Motsch in 1974. Motsch moved on, but Rice kept the studio going, doing primarily work for retail clients for the next ten years. She then branched out and now handles print projects for a wide variety of clients. In 1990, Rice's husband, Dick, joined the studio. Dick graduated from Indiana University and had worked in the printing and forms industry for fifteen years. About 75 percent of his current work is customized form design. Today Artworks operates out of an old, restored farmhouse, where the main floor is "full of computers" and meeting rooms for working with and presenting to clients.

Vicki and Dick Rice's studio, Artworks, has grown by helping clients, both for profit and nonprofit, grow. Both have clients of their own; much of Dick's work is customized form design, since his background is in the printing and forms business. Vicki's background is design for retail operations; she started her career as art director for the Paul Harris Stores chain after graduating from John Herron School of Art in Indianapolis.

They collaborate on direct mail projects and one huge project, a three-hundred-page Russian guidebook/telephone directory that is published twice a year. The Rices were approached by an Indiana businessman, who had been struck by the lack of telephone directories or yellow pages in the far eastern section of Russia. (The area is *nine* hours from Moscow by plane.) The businessman proposed to remedy that lack, a project that he believed would be quite profitable for both himself and the directory's publisher. The Rices design and handle production work on the directory; their client adds the Russian translation of all copy. The phone directory even includes a full-color advertising section, mainly promoting tourism. (One ad that caught Vicki's attention advertised a fresh, clearwater lake the size of Indiana.) Their work on the telephone directory resulted in a consulting agreement between Artworks and Vladivostok Graphics.

Artworks frequently benefits from client-to-client referrals. The studio has a knack for getting on board with small, local companies, whose businesses have subsequently taken off. The Rices have found this kind of work to be particularly exciting— and rewarding. One client, Design Industries, makes what Vicki enthusiastically describes as "wonderful store fixturing." This client had done little promotion before coming to the Rices for a logo and, later, some print ads. Although Design Industries has now grown much larger, with Eddie Bauer and Banana Republic among their customers, they're still an Artworks client. Another client that started with them while still a small, local business is Putting Greens International, which sells small putting greens for homes and hotels. After being in business only five years, this client has signed international deals in South Africa, Venezuela and Sweden. The owner of the business credits Artworks for helping them grow.

The "K-9 Walk for MDA" is an example of work for a pro bono client. Vicki, a dog lover, couldn't resist when she was asked to do the graphics for this annual event. These "dog walks" are held in cities all over the United States under the sponsorship of local chapters of the Muscular Dystrophy Association. The Indianapolis chapter admits it owes much of its success—it's now the largest K-9 walk in the country—to Vicki's warm and winning graphics. MDA chapters in Kentucky and Tennessee have asked Vicki's permission to use her graphics, too. The national organization is delighted, because big sponsors such as Pro-Plan Dog Food gladly come aboard when shown the graphics used in Indianapolis. These and other success stories show how both studio and client can benefit when a good idea or product is combined with good design.

"K-9 Walk for MDA" Poster, Flyer and T-Shirt
Design: Vicki L. Rice
Printing: Poster and flyer: White Arts, Inc.
T-Shirt: silkscreened by Burrittos Silkscreen
Quantity: 600 posters; 15,000 flyers; 900 T-shirts
Budget: Posters: primarily donated
Flyers: donated
T-Shirts: partially donated

The Indianapolis K-9 Walk has developed into the biggest in the country. The national Muscular Dystrophy Association has used Rice's graphics as examples of how to entice potential sponsors into supporting the events, and other MDA chapters have since contacted Rice. Everything for the posters was donated, except the paper, which was purchased at cost. As for the T-shirts, the artwork was donated, while the shirts themselves were supplied and printed at a discounted price. There's continuity from year to year, with a few additions to the cast of mutts and new colors to keep the promotions looking fresh.

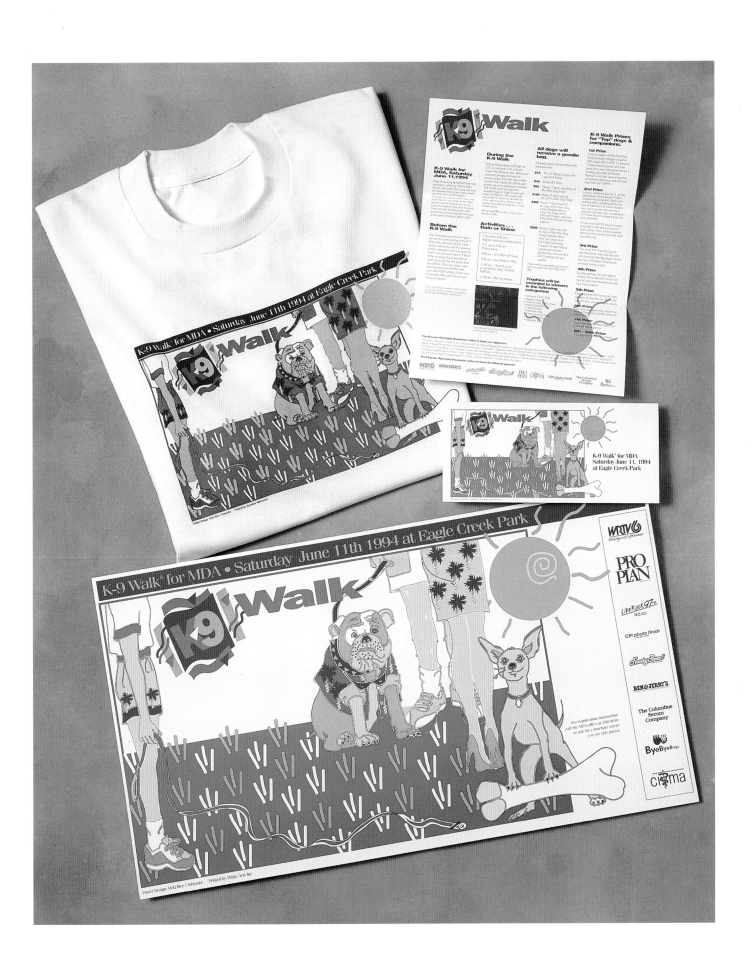

John Evans Design Contributing Creatively

John Evans Design is based in Dallas; Evans lives in Plano, Texas, with his wife, Laurie, and their two children, Jacqueline and Zachary. Evans received a Bachelor of Fine Arts Degree from the Art Center College of Design in Pasadena, California. He specializes in corporate identity, packaging, illustration and advertising. Evans has taught a graphic design class at East Texas State University since 1990. His client list includes Milton Bradley, American Airlines, Parker Brothers, Mary Kay Cosmetics, GTE, Frito Lay, the American Heart Association and Quaker Oats. His work has appeared in Print, Graphis, Communication Arts, *the New York Art Directors Club show, American Institute of the Graphic Arts, the Dallas Society of Visual Communications and the Los Angeles Art Directors Club.*

John Evans considers his pro bono work his contribution to his community. "With two small children, and another one due any day," he says, "I don't have time to work at a soup kitchen." If the cause is worthwhile, Evans is glad to contribute his design work. Evans has done a number of logos for local nonprofit organizations. Clients or printers sometimes recommend him for these pro bono projects. However, Evans asks that the organizations solicit their own printing. If he asked the printers for such favors, he'd feel he personally owed the printers some work. Although Evans does pro bono work as a way of giving to others, he receives a lot of creative freedom in return. Many of his pro bono logos have found their way into design annuals and competitions.

Evans also does logos for agencies, which are constantly in need of logos for advertising campaigns. Although Dallas has a lot of small design studios, many working for the same clients, there is a lot of agency—and other—work to go around. The logos Evans does for agencies aren't always the sort of project you put in your portfolio, but he has gotten some neat logo and menu projects from them. These generally quick-in/quick-out jobs do pay well, and there aren't client meetings. Sketches are often faxed back and forth.

A logo book promotion (see page 105) mainly targets the agencies. Evans would like to do another logo book in a year or two and a Christmas card every year. His promotion plans are modest because he is "extremely happy with where I am."

The Mayor's Summit on Juvenile Violence

PACT (Parents and Children Together)

The Women's Shelter

Pro Bono Logos
Design: John Evans
Budget: Design donated
Evans's logos have assisted a wide variety of local causes. He enjoys these pro bono projects, which give him a chance to contribute to the community and to enjoy creative freedom.

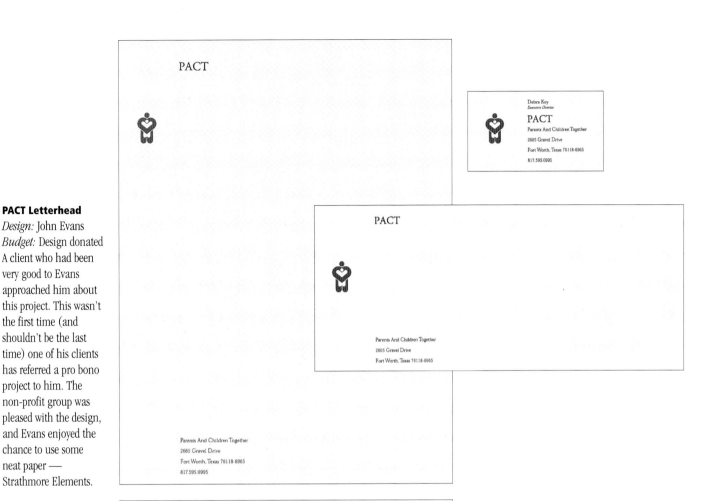

PACT Letterhead

Design: John Evans
Budget: Design donated
A client who had been very good to Evans approached him about this project. This wasn't the first time (and shouldn't be the last time) one of his clients has referred a pro bono project to him. The non-profit group was pleased with the design, and Evans enjoyed the chance to use some neat paper — Strathmore Elements.

Community Forum on Character and Values Stationery

Design: John Evans
Quantity: 2,500
Budget: Design donated
Both clients and printers refer pro bono projects to Evans, because they know he'll gladly lend his time to a worthwhile cause. This project came through Padgett Printing, the company that donated the printing for Evans's logo book promotion. (See page 105.) There were few creative or production limits imposed.

Christmas Card

Design: John Evans
Quantity: 150
Budget: $100 (printing)
These cards were silkscreened by one of Evans's students at East Texas State University. They were sent to both clients and family.

Christmas Card

Design: John Evans
Illustration: Jacqueline Evans, age 4
Quantity: 250
Budget: $150 (printing)
Evans liked the idea of working as a father/daughter team on this card. He appreciates the quality of children's illustration, and notes, "They do it so easily."

Wedding Announcement

Design: John Evans
Quantity: 1,500
Budget: Design donated
This new take on the traditional wedding advice to have "something old, something new, something borrowed, something blue" is actually a combination wedding announcement and invitation to the July 3rd reception: "something red, white and blue." It was designed for a friend who is a paper rep. The printing and paper were donated. The colorful visuals began life as public domain engravings.

Logo Book

Design: John Evans

Quantity: 500

Budget: Printing donated

Evans's paper rep showed him the cover paper and then worked with the printer on the piece. Evans used the short sheets at the front to add color to the two-color printing inside. The printer suggested the solid red ink for the left-hand pages.

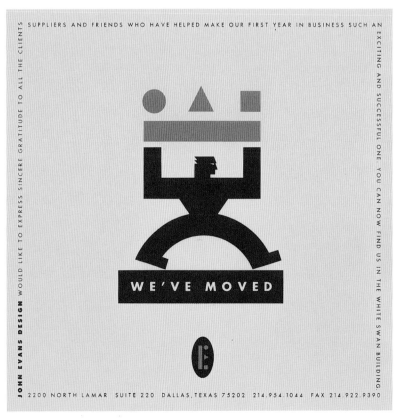

Evans's Moving Announcement

Design: John Evans

Quantity: 150

Budget: $100 (printing)

Evans had leftover square envelopes from his Christmas cards. He mailed this two-color card (red and black inks on yellow stock) to clients, suppliers and friends. The "moving man" is carrying the *E* symbol from Evans's logo.

D. Betz Design Both Parties Can Benefit

D. Betz Design is a multi-disciplinary design office. Originally established in Cincinnati, in 1990, Betz decided to relocate to Seattle in the fall of 1993. The studio has worked with a diverse group of clients across the country, from museums, commercial real estate developers and retailers to publishers, software companies and on-line service companies. His client list includes Formica Corp., Gourmet Furniture, Integra Technology, U. S. Shoe Corp., the Cincinnati Symphony, the Cousteau Society, the Contemporary Arts Center (Cincinnati), and the Virginia Beach Center for the Arts. The work of D. Betz Design has been published nationally and internationally in Graphis, Communication Arts, HOW, Print, Graphis Poster 94, *and* Letterheads 2. *It is also part of the archival collection at Columbia University.*

At its best, pro bono work can be a situation where everybody wins. A nonprofit or an organization with limited resources gets great graphics at little or no cost, the designer gets far more creative freedom than can be found in day-to-day projects, and the community benefits from these thriving charitable and art organizations. That's how it should be, but often it isn't.

Many designers have cut back on or stopped doing pro bono work entirely. Some have found themselves inundated with more requests than they can handle without dropping better-paying work. Others, sadly, cite difficulty in receiving the designer's half of the bargain—creative freedom in exchange for their donated services. In an era of dwindling donations and funding problems, other groups feel that they can't take creative risks anymore, because people might be turned off by a particular piece and withdraw their financial support. Still other organizations are headed by large, volunteer boards of directors (who must all pass judgment) or may have staff with their own creative egos that can get in the way of good design.

But designers who can make their way through the approval maze are doing work that brings support to the nonprofit client and awards to their studios, while providing a service to the community. And, while it isn't always true, there are still many nonprofits who encourage designers, illustrators, photographers and other artists to "push the envelope" of creativity.

David Betz, who has done a number of award-winning pro bono pieces for clients, says the secret of his success is finding a design advocate on the client's board or staff. Although D. Betz Design relocated from Cincinnati to Seattle, Betz continues to work with the Cincinnati Contemporary Arts Center (CAC), where Carolyn Krause, the director of publications, understands and supports the value of good design. Jan Riley, formerly with the CAC, joined the Virginia Beach Art Center and has built a coast-to-coast relationship with D. Betz Design. Both Krause and Riley feel that the work Betz does not only enhances the images of their organizations but also pays off in raising awareness and community support.

Betz promotes himself to business clients by stressing his problem-solving abilities; concept is very important in his work. He sends tearsheets and photocopies of his work with thoughtful letters that support his main thesis—good design is good business.

"Mechanika" Catalog
Design: David Betz
Photography: Ron Forth
Quantity: 2,000
Budget: Design donated
Betz designed this catalog for an exhibit on the machine and art for Cincinnati's Contemporary Arts Center (CAC). CAC had just presented a controversial exhibit of Robert Mapplethorpe's photographs. To show his support, Betz went to the CAC and said, "I want to do something for you." They didn't have a project then, but three months later Carolyn Krause and Jan Riley called with "Mechanika." The book has won numerous awards and was one of only eight books chosen by the AIGA to be included in the prestigious exhibit, "The Best Designed Books From All Over the World," at the Frankfurt Book Fair.

CAC Overview (Five Years' Worth of Nonprofit Work)
Design: David Betz
Illustration: David Betz
Photography: Barry Gregg
Quantity: 1
Budget: $30 to dupe existing pieces
As a thank-you to the Contemporary Arts Center (CAC), Betz assembled a collage documenting the work he had done for them. He uses the photograph of this collage in his portfolio and has also sent slides of the piece to arts organizations for whom he would like to work to lend credibility and to serve as a reminder of all the successful projects he has done.

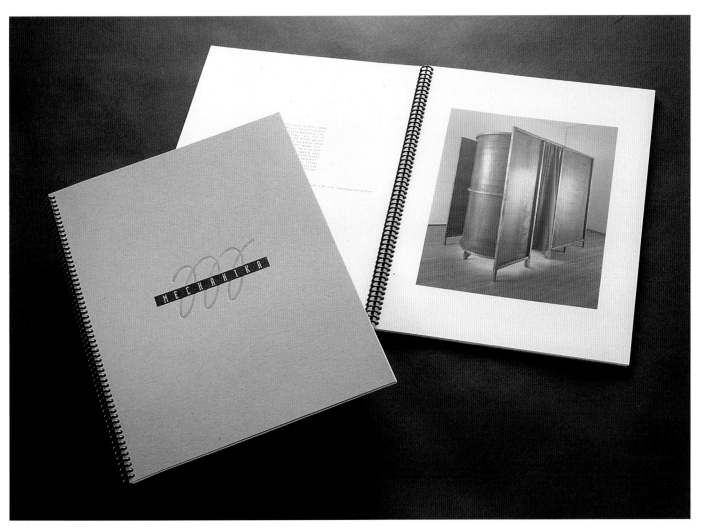

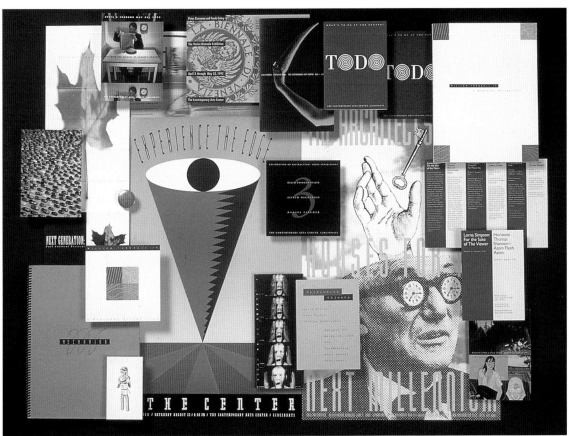

Day of the Dead Postcard

Design: David Betz
Photography: David Betz
Quantity: 2,500
Budget: Design donated

This postcard promoted a benefit dance party held by the Virginia Beach Center for the Arts. The party was scheduled for October 29, or the *Dia de Muertos* (Day of the Dead). Betz purchased the toy skulls, photographed them on a paper background, and separated the image from a "corner drugstore print." He still wishes it could have been done as a poster. He's mounted it eight-up for effect in his studio.

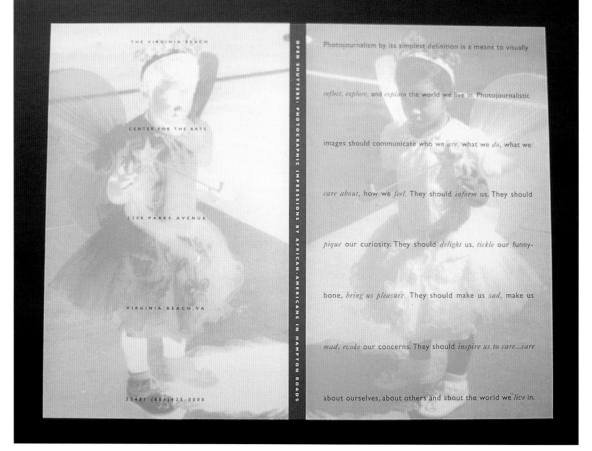

Open Shutters Catalog

Design: David Betz
Photography: Various amateur photographers from Hampton Roads
Quantity: 1,000
Budget: Design donated

This catalog accompanies an exhibit of the work of amateur photographers; these photos were created as part of an outreach program in disadvantaged Hampton Roads, Virginia.

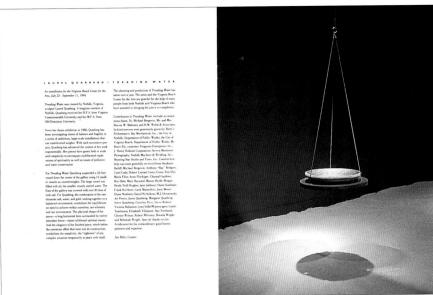

Laurel Quarberg: Treading Water Catalog

Design: David Betz
Photography: Brenda Wright
Editor: Victoria L. Robinson
Curator (of exhibit): Jan Riley
Quantity: 2,500
Budget: Design donated

This exhibition catalog was printed and distributed while the exhibition was still running — a rare occurrence in the art world.

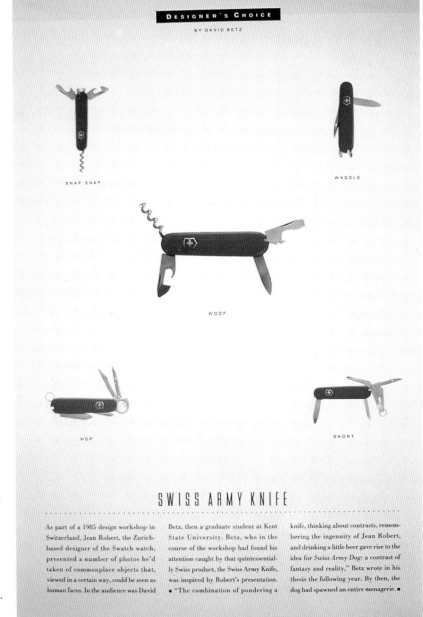

Swiss Army Knife Book

Design: David Betz
Photography: Brad Logan
Quantity: 27
Budget: Design donated

This concept was originally the basis for Betz's thesis for his Master of Fine Arts degree at Kent State University. Without any funding for printing, Betz printed a limited edition letterpress book, *Swiss Army Dog,* himself. Five years later, an editor at *Graphis* who had heard about the project wanted to run the images in a column featuring the actual art. Betz found a similar knife and got a photographer friend, Brad Logan, to shoot the knife in its various shapes. The print piece ran in *Graphis.*

CopperLeaf Pro Bono Publishing

CopperLeaf Studio (formerly Gryphon III Design) is a Columbus, Ohio, studio specializing in design for publishing and advertising companies. The two principals are Cathleen Carbery and Stephen Shaw. Carbery has an extensive background in design and illustration with twelve years' experience in publishing. She worked for specialty publisher F&W Publications in Cincinnati, Ohio, before relocating to Columbus, where she worked for the text-book division of Macmillan Publishing. Shaw brings a high level of computer skills to the design team. He worked as a composite engineer on projects utilizing computer-aided design for Dow United Technologies. He was also a partner in Interactive Images, creating three-dimensional images and advertising graphics.

Columbus, Ohio, is a growing city with a small town atmosphere. Personable and enthusiastic, Cathleen Carbery is well known in the local artistic community and has done pro bono design work for Buckeye Boys Ranch, Ronald McDonald House, and Big Brothers and Sisters. She attributes the success of CopperLeaf to good, old-fashioned networking.

Carbery and partner Stephen Shaw want to do more publishing work. That's Carbery's forte (with twelve years' experience in that industry), and Shaw brings complementary production skills from his background in computer-based design technologies. He worked with a color imaging company and has extensive experience in color scanning, color separation and prepress. The prospect of large, complex, text-heavy projects aren't as intimidating as they might be for another studio.

So, it seemed a good fit when they were asked to publish the cookbook, *Ronald McDonald House of NYC Cookbook* by Ronald McDonald House. Sales of these cookbooks would finance many of the organization's activities in the coming year. In addition to seeing the project from initial development to printing, CopperLeaf became the book's actual publisher — even supplying an official ISBN number. This let the non-profit organization get the cookbook into bookstores for general sale to supplement their direct and mail order efforts.

CopperLeaf's second pro bono publishing project, *Star Chefs: 1994*, for the local March of Dimes, shows that success breeds success. Armed with their recent experience in taking a book from idea to production, Carbery and Shaw brought the new project to a happy conclusion. The cookbooks provided not only the chance to do something for their community, they also provided promotional opportunities. The studio got samples of the books to use for their self-promotion, and sent a number of them to potential clients in New York City, where much book publishing is done.

The Ronald McDonald House of NYC Cookbook

Art Direction: Cathleen Carbery
Design: Cathleen Carbery
Illustration: Cathleen Carbery
Quantity: 25,000
Budget: Design donated

The Ronald McDonald House is a "home away from home" for families of children being treated for cancer. This project gave CopperLeaf some valuable exposure in the New York area and helped to forward a very worthwhile cause.

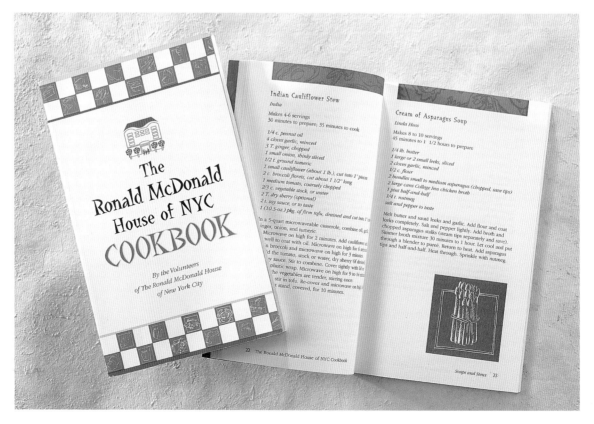

**Star Chefs: 1994
Book of Recipes**

Art Direction: Cathleen
Carbery

Design: Cathleen
Carbery

Photography:
Cunningham/
Feinknopf
Photography

Quantity: 15,000

Budget: Design donated
The *Star Chefs* cookbook is the official text companion to the Columbus March of Dimes annual gourmet auction. This event, a combination dinner and live auction fund-raiser, benefits the local March of Dimes. The book also benefitted CopperLeaf, leading directly to one large catalog job and increasing their overall exposure in the community.

Handmade Book and Bookmark

Design: Cathleen Carbery

Quantity: 60

Budget: $300

Carbery and Shaw assembled this handmade book to serve as a portfolio piece. Quotes from satisfied clients alternate with illustrations of projects the studio has handled. The type comes from the studio's laser printer while the illustrations are color photocopies of the book jackets done on a Canon color photocopier. A friend who had studied bookbinding helped Carbery and Shaw produce the books, which are held together with copper-colored posts. This makes it easy to change the piece as needed and helped keep both production costs and assembly time to a reasonable amount.

Art Chantry Creating a Conduit for Communication

Art Chantry started doing graphic design in high school, mainly psychedelic logos for guitar shops. Raised in the Northwest, he spent some time in London, before returning to Seattle in 1980 to do his thing. His striking posters and other promotional work for a diverse group of artists and arts organizations have brought him awards as well as the satisfaction of bringing some unusual performers to the attention of mainstream audiences.

A self-taught designer, Art Chantry was first a fan of comic books and posters, then immersed himself in art history. He was particularly affected by dadaism and surrealism. He pursues graphic design as an art form and sees it in an archeological context as a product of our culture, or "folk art for a technological society." Chantry sees the fine art world as a small subculture with a limited audience. He tries to reach out to a wider audience with his art. He has ties to some unusual subcultures that, incidentally, feel he is pretty mainstream. Chantry acts as a conduit for those groups whose visual language has a limited audience, helping them communicate with a larger audience that finds the imagery startling—but ultimately intriguing.

Chantry's success in creating unusual, visual vocabularies is reflected in the number of designs that reflect (or even copy) his style. He used to feel ripped off when he saw his visual approach appropriated by others, but now he sees the imitation of ideas as part of the communication process. Chantry pushes for iconographic meaning in his works, for something that communicates in a universal way. In fact, he says one of his goals is to anonymously develop the next "happy face" — a symbol or icon that becomes an integral, ubiquitous element of popular culture.

He likes getting a reaction, so he avoids the obvious solution, seeking instead some way "to throw a monkey wrench into the process." Even mistakes on press or bad printing can produce interesting results. Since he doesn't handle the printing for much of his work, there are often interesting, unintended results. Chantry uses chewed-up press type and grainy photocopies in much of his work. He feels that clean, slick type and art off the computer is now so easy to do that it's become an obvious solution to be avoided.

Chantry used to think he wanted corporate clients, but he now believes he's not the "group think" kind of person that such clients want. He enjoys the work he does, although he'd like to get paid more for doing it. He gets a small credit line on his posters and says, "Without that line, nobody would know who I was at all." Thanks, in part, to those credit lines, however, Chantry is now very well known indeed.

Clients seek out Chantry because they like his radical approach. He recently completed an advertising insert for Urban Outfitters. Aiming for what he describes as the "jolt factor," Chantry designed the insert to look like a 1950s tool catalog. He says there was such a contrast between the "pretty editorial and the other unobtrusive pretty ads and the Urban Outfitters' insert" that the piece divides the magazine visually in half.

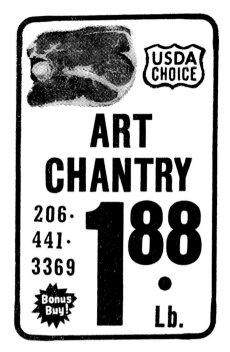

Self-Promotion Ad
Design: Art Chantry
Budget: $500
Chantry was approached to do some of the design work for a new black book, a directory of design professionals. He was given a page at a reduced rate in return. He says he was sure that nothing else in the book would look remotely like his page.

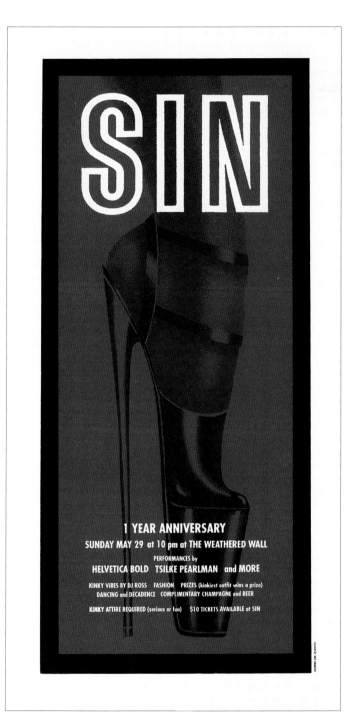

Sin Poster
Design: Art Chantry
Quantity: 200
Budget: $100 (printing paid by client)
Sin, a fetish clothing store, celebrated its first anniversary with a party featuring music by local rock groups. Chantry's poster was so popular that the store hired him to design their catalog and work on in-store merchandising.

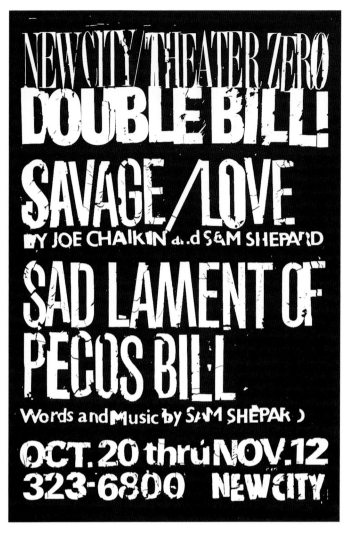

New City/Theater Zero Poster
Design: Art Chantry
Quantity: 300
Budget: $400
Chantry has long been a fan of Norman LaLiberty, an early member of Pushpin, and his experimental work with press type. This piece illustrates not only Chantry's respect for LaLiberty's work but also a reaction against the universal, clean, immaculately polished look of type from the computer. It's almost impossible to duplicate on a computer the crooked, broken quality of the press type used here.

Earth Police Badge
Design: Art Chantry, Dana Lyons
Quantity: 100
Budget: Design donated
One of Chantry's friends asked him to design a logo for badges to be used by a loosely knit group of "alternative Boy Scouts" protecting the earth.

Kustom Kulture Poster
Design: Art Chantry
Printing: Art Garcia
Quantity: 100
Budget: Design donated
Chantry is a fan of hot rod culture. He says that Von Dutch was the first graphic artist to silkscreen a T-shirt, and Ed Roth did the first silkscreen designs in fluorescent colors. For this piece, Chantry wanted to do justice to the men who invented flame jobs and pinstriping with a look that can best be described as "*Popular Mechanics* meets hot rods." Artist Art Garcia, who works for the printer, also appreciates hot rod art. He brought his own artistry to the project.

Hempfest Posters

Design: Art Chantry and Jamie Sheehan

Quantity: 500 on hemp burlap, 500 on hemp paper

Budget: Design donated

Chantry worked with young designer Sheehan on this poster promoting a free concert and fund-raiser. The poster was printed on 100 percent hemp burlap and 100 percent hemp paper. Chantry promotes the use of these substances as alternatives to printing on traditional wood pulp paper. He says that an acre of hemp produces as much paper as five acres of timberland and is a renewable resource.

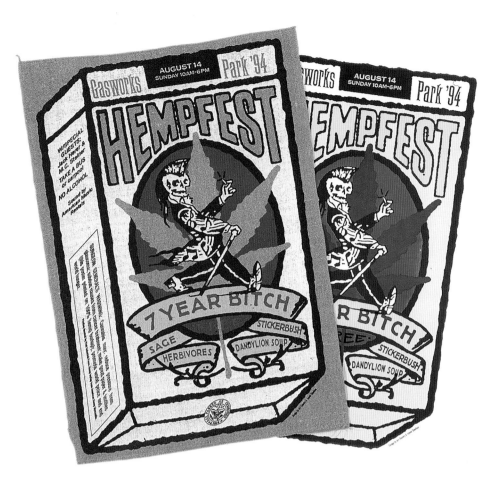

Bullseye Poster

Design: Art Chantry

Printing: BSK(T)

Quantity: 150

Budget: Design donated

This poster promotes a fund-raising concert for Hands Off Washington — groups opposed to the Oregon Citizens Alliance (OCA). Since OCA, which opposes gay rights, "targets" gays, Chantry arranged the type in a bullseye. The figure in the background was enlarged several times. Chantry likes the distortion that occurs in an image after multiple reproductions.

Collaborating for Promotional Success

Collaboration most often means working with a photographer, illustrator or printer, but it can also include mutually beneficial working relationships with a paper company, a color separator or a binder. And the possibilities don't end there.

Even two separate design studios can benefit from collaborating rather than competing. Amy Quinlivan and Sharon Werner are great examples of this, with an informal partnership that allows them to work on individual projects, or joint projects, as the situation calls for.

The only rule that applies in all cases is this: Everyone involved should benefit from the project in some way. As long as that's true, no one will feel the resentment that can come from being "taken advantage of," all parties will be motivated to treat the project seriously, and the end result will be something everyone can be happy with.

Peterson & Co. Working Relationships

Peterson & Co. is a full-service graphic design firm recognized nationally for corporate communications and college recruitment publications. Founded in 1985 by Bryan Peterson, the studio has grown to seven employees and a client base that includes Centex, Frito-Lay, Mothers Against Drunk Driving, Northern Telecom and PepsiCo, Inc. College clientele includes Columbia University, Emory & Henry College, New York University, Southern Methodist University and the University of Texas at Dallas. Two of the company's posters have been chosen by the Library of Congress for its permanent collection of graphic design. The staff's work has appeared in Communication Arts, Graphis Annual Reports, Print *magazine, and the* Society of Publication Designers Annual.

Successful working relationships among its staff as well as with clients and fellow creative professionals are the hallmark of Peterson & Co. The five art director/designers have the freedom to act autonomously, but none of the headaches of being in business for themselves. Each designer art directs, manages and schedules his or her own projects, including working with clients. Bryan Peterson and his staff have also developed strong working relationships with many other creative professionals and can provide clients with the services of experienced writers, printers, photographers and illustrators.

Although the concept and specific goal of each project varies, all the studio's promotional efforts must accomplish one of three things:

- allow the studio staff to expand their design abilities;
- directly promote the studio; or
- lead to new work with an existing or potential client.

The studio's staff bring their extensive knowledge of production and printing to the aid of some of their low-budget clients, looking for every efficiency and opportunity to get the most out of limited project budgets. The studio collaborated with photographer Ric Moore and South Press on a pro bono brochure for the YMCA that had to look very upscale on a minuscule budget. Warm duotones and spot color give the piece sophisti-

cation without a lot of cost. Peterson & Company bring that same, effective but sensible approach to the studio's self-promotion, and even to collaborative efforts such as *Rough* (a publication of the Dallas Society of Visual Communications) and promotions with other creative professionals.

Bryan Peterson and photographer Robb Debenport have worked together for years. When Debenport approached Peterson about designing a brochure, Peterson drew on his connections for a separator and printer who would donate their services for a prominent credit. The binder agreed to donate his services to show off his new flat-lay binding process. Peterson also arranged to have the paper donated in exchange for samples. Unfortunately, this increased the size of the print run and the work for the printer and bindery—who were persuaded to do the additional work by assurances that the greater exposure would be worth it.

Peterson also collaborated on a brochure with photographer John Wong. Wong initially asked him to do his letterhead. Peterson jokingly suggested a concept depicting photography as Wong's last resort for a career, after egg roll wrapper and Chinese launderer had been crossed off. Wong liked the idea, because it showed he had a sense of humor; in fact, he liked it so well, they expanded the idea from small visuals on a letterhead to a whole brochure.

Downtown Dallas YMCA Brochure

Art Direction: Nhan Pham

Design: Nhan Pham

Photography: Ric Moore

Printing: South Press

Quantity: 10,000

Budget: $8,200

The YMCA didn't have a lot of money, but they needed an upscale design reminiscent of annual reports that would be attractive to the target audience of executives. Peterson & Co. and photographer Ric Moore did this project as a joint effort. The rich, warm duotones and use of spot color give the piece a sophisticated look without the expense of four-color separations.

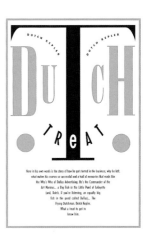

November '94 Issue of Rough

Art Direction: Jan Wilson

Design: Jan Wilson, Dave Eliason, Bryan Peterson, Nhan Pham

Quantity: 2,500

Budget: $150

Rough is a publication of the Dallas Society of Visual Communications. All printing, design, photography and illustration are donated. For the two issues that Peterson & Co. designed and produced (September and November), one designer acted as art director and assigned stories to the others. They also had to work fast—the schedule called for design and production in under two weeks for each issue.

Robb Debenport Photography Brochure

Art Direction: Bryan Peterson
Photography: Robb Debenport
Quantity: 22,000
Budget: Design donated

This brochure was designed to showcase the photographer's work, but much more went into it than great photographs and a strong design. Peterson persuaded a separator and a printer to donate their services, and a binder agreed to donate his services to show off his new, flat-lay binding process. Peterson then asked Mohawk if they would donate the paper. Mohawk agreed, because Peterson had often specified the company's papers, but they did ask for numerous copies in return, pushing the run to 22,000. Peterson, who had coordinated the effort, added a dedication to the teamwork that had contributed so much to the brochure.

John Wong Photography Brochure

Art Direction: Bryan Peterson
Design: Bryan Peterson
Photography: John Wong
Quantity: 2,500
Budget: $5,000

To control costs on this brochure, John Wong got all of the props and did the set-up. Peterson designed the brochure as a sixteen-page booklet, so it could fit on one sheet. The rich halftone quality is achieved by careful exposure of the prints, delicate balance by the stripper of the overall tones (with 3 percent and lighter printing white), 95 percent in the blacks, and rich, full mid-ranges in between. This involved dodging and burning by the separator and careful printing.

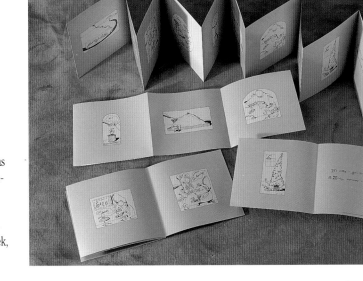

Christmas Card

Art Direction: Scott Ray
Design: Scott Ray
Illustration: Keith Graves
Printing: South Press
Quantity: 150
Budget: $450

Scott Ray was brainstorming ideas for a Christmas promotion on the theme of recycling, when someone mentioned the ultimate recycled gift—fruitcakes. Scott reasoned that the same fruitcake is often passed on to others. Illustrator Keith Graves worked in his doodle style for this tongue-in-cheek, three-color, one-sided piece.

Christmas Invitation

Art Direction: Scott Ray
Design: Scott Ray
Assembly: Peterson & Co.
Printing: South Press
Quantity: 150
Budget: $450

Scott Ray purchased the Santa hats (from a large grocery store chain) and standard mailing tubes. He and the other Peterson & Co. staffers wrapped the tubes in dimpled, super kraft paper that had been debossed and trimmed out at the printer. Then they added the label, "Put on Your Party Hats." The result resembles a more expensive custom tube. Ray drilled holes in the plastic tops of the tubes, so they could pull through the fluffy, white ball on the top of the hat. It took roughly one day to assemble the invitations.

ADAI Poster

Art Direction: Bryan Peterson
Design: Bryan Peterson
Photography: John Wong
Quantity: 500
Budget: Design donated

Bryan Peterson was invited to speak to the ADAI in Iowa not long after the floods in the Midwest. By the time he spoke, the subject was no longer a sensitive one, so the ADAI okayed a poster with a flood theme. John Wong shot the designer's tools as Polaroids which Peterson then scanned into the computer and distorted with a wave filter in Adobe Photoshop. Peterson then bitmapped and positioned them for the poster.

Tom Bonauro Pure Creativity

Tom Bonauro has been working independently as a graphic designer in San Francisco for about fifteen years. He currently has a full-time designer, John Choe, on staff. The studio's projects include advertising, identity systems and packaging. Bonauro also directs film and videos. Bonauro's work has been featured in publications ranging from ID, HOW *and* Print *to* Interview *and* Vanity Fair. *His clients include Apple Computer, Todd Oldham (for whom he designed packaging for a line of fragrances), Levis, Esprit, MTV, Warner Bros. and A&M Records. Bonauro has also designed a Swatch watch.*

Tom Bonauro developed his design aesthetic while studying fine art and art history. This same artistic aesthetic also drives his self-promotions. Bonauro's self-promotion has evolved from some pieces he describes as "minimal" to the books he now does.

He approaches these self-promotions as opportunities to work on "dream projects." Instead of having the primary objective of marketing a product or announcing an event, his promotions have as their primary objective pure creativity.

Many of the visuals in Bonauro's books are, or are developed from, photos he gets for trade from local photographers. Some of the photography is manipulated in Photoshop with the photographer's consent. He also uses found images.

In addition to fine art and art history, Bonauro studied printmaking and later applied that knowledge to offset printing. He has worked with the same printer, Logos Graphics, for ten years, and says they work closely on projects on a basis that is more collaborative than many printer/designer relationships. Bonauro does press

checks, and he and the printer often make changes on press. All of Bonauro's promotions were printed by this same printer. For the *He Went Through the Rocks* book, the panel in the back of the book was done as a version change, so the printer could use the book for his own self-promotion.

Bonauro has carefully developed a mailing list of artists and some agencies he thinks will respond to the aesthetic of his promotions. They have been well received. The Cooper-Hewitt Museum has asked for additional copies of his books for their collection, and the Museum of Modern Art in San Francisco is also collecting his work. Bonauros' work was also shown in the History of Graphic Design exhibit, and at Pratt Institute in a show on typography, architecture and design.

A Feeling in Your Bones Book

Art Direction: Tom Bonauro
Design: Tom Bonauro
Quantity: 1,000
Budget: $2,000
Bonauro's credit and address are printed on the wrapper. This book also served as a promo for the printer, who shared the costs.

He Went Through the Rocks Book

Art Direction: Tom Bonauro
Design: Tom Bonauro, John Choe
Quantity: 1,000
Budget: $2,000
This book was done in collaboration with the printer, Logos Graphics. They split the cost of the paper, and the printer did a version change on one page, so they could also use the book as a printing promotion.

Amy Quinlivan Design Creative Collaboration, Creative Freedom

Amy Quinlivan opened her graphic design studio in Minneapolis after seven years with Dayton/Hudson and a year working with Werner Jeker's Atelier Du Nord in Lausanne, Switzerland. Her projects include retail advertising, direct mail, product development, packaging and signage, book design and corporate communications. Her work has been recognized with awards and honors and has appeared in British Design and Art Direction, Print, Communication Arts, Adweek, Graphic Design USA, HOW *and the American Center for Design 100 Show. Among her clients are several retailers — Target, Bloomingdales, Dayton/Hudson, and the Musicland Group — as well as Nike, Sony Music, Trident Medical International, Hershey Communications and Viacom/VH-1.*

Amy Quinlivan Design, Inc. has a rather unusual collaborative relationship with Sharon Werner of Werner Design Werks. They often work together on projects, but are not a partnership in any formal business sense. Quinlivan and Werner have watched traditional design partnerships break up and feel that such an arrangement would be too restrictive for them.

But both women came from larger creative environments and missed the creative give-and-take available there. They both enjoy their collaborative efforts and give each other valuable feedback on both individual and joint projects. Since Werner Design Werks and Quinlivan Design are small shops, they benefit more from being allies than competitors.

Werner and Quinlivan may not always agree on the best creative approach to a project—one may favor a photographic solution, the other a typographic one—but they work out their differences in the best interest of the client. On several occasions, that client has been themselves, as when they teamed up for a four-part poster series that promoted both studios. The series has been recognized by the Design 100 Show, the New York Art Directors Club and *Graphis*, although Quinlivan notes that some of their clients didn't understand it. This didn't bother them too much, however, since the piece was never envisioned as a mass mailing. It was primarily targeted to creatives and potential clients with a strong interest in creative work, such as VH-1.

AMY QUINLIVAN *Design* 612 · 341 · 8226

AQ Postcard
Design: Amy Quinlivan
Quantity: 300
Budget: $200
Quinlivan designed the postcard so she could just pick up the film work from her identity system. She had a single line of type set and then had a duotone made by Rapid Print.

Beauty, Simplicity and Economy Folder

Design: Amy Quinlivan
Photography: Glen Gyssler, Mike Habermann
Printing: Northstar
Quantity: 1,500
Budget: Minimal—trim and scoring

This accordion folder was printed on the trim space
of a job Quinlivan was designing for a large retailer.
The photos were existing images from the photographers' portfolios. Gyssler and Habermann agreed to
let her use them in exchange for a credit on the
piece.

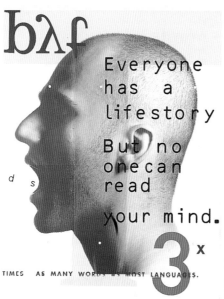

**Words Four-Part
Poster Series**

Design: Amy Quinlivan,
  Sharon Werner
Photographer: Mike
  Crousser
Printer: Printcraft
Typesetting: Great Faces
Quantity: 4,000
Budget: $0

This four-part poster
series was used to pro-
mote both Amy
Quinlivan Design and
Werner Design Werks. It
was a collaborative
effort not only between
the two studios but also
with the printer and the
typehouse. The only cost
to Quinlivan and
Werner was their time.

Everyone
has a
lifestory

But no
one can
read

your mind.

3x

TIMES AS MANY WORDS AS MOST LANGUAGES.

Words.
The table of contents
Melting pot of polyglo
Lexicon of our lives.
Skywritten. Scrabbled.
Take a letter, Maria. I
Words, the street sign
Incantation. Expletive.
The borders of Bodoni
the confines of Futura
futile foil for undulati
Body and soul. Vellum
Words get under your
Every one secretes we

1. amy quinlivan design
2. werner design werks inc.
3. print craft inc.
4. great faces inc.

for culture.

t.

In script. Or tattoo.
P.S. I love you.
s where we live.

Condensed

VWMNK
OCSQGA
XYZIEFL
UDBRP
JTH;,!?
567891 23

communicate

ENGLISH HAS   THREE

to the letter

put it
in your own
words.

A-Z

Each choice. A voice.
Ballpoint bombast. Bl
Unilateral treaty or d
Word as adhesion and
Slang, the ace flung u
Linguistic elixir. Imbi
Utterance. Eloquence.
Take away words and
justice wouldn't be po
Ideas and dreams wou
You couldn't get it in
You'd never have the
ons within.
or scroll.
skin.
t ink.
The way you think.
ckboard. Braille.
aily mail.
ancestry.
p its sleeve.
ed and expelled.
Curses. Do tell.
etic.
ld be deterred.
writing.
last word.

Straight Face Studio Shared Resources, Shared Benefits

Working together as partners, Kenn Tompos and Leslie Jaffe started Straight Face Studio in 1990. Tompos now works alone, specializing in publications, but he also takes on a wide range of projects that include annual reports, identity projects, and marketing and sales communications for corporations and small businesses.

For trade-outs to work, everyone involved has to benefit. That was definitely the case on this collaborative self-promotion. Photographer David Clark Wendt wanted an opportunity to get exposure for personal work not often seen by his clients in order to open new markets. Kenn Tompos agreed to design the project in exchange for creative freedom and some copies of the poster he could use as leave-behinds. Tompos felt he could have some fun with this unusual project and get a nice leave-behind for his Straight Face Studio in the bargain.

Tompos's design for the project was inspired by the photos themselves. He and Wendt chose three images that could be combined to tell a story; other elements were then added to fill it out. The "Audible

Imagery" tagline came from various sounds associated with trains. Tompos says it "relates to the way great photography can trigger memories from senses besides sight."

The photographer traded the use of some images to the separator/printer, who wanted to do a self-promotion featuring his seven-color press, in exchange for the work. The paper was provided at a special discount and free for overruns in exchange for copies of the poster. The primary stock was Quintessence Dull, but one hundred each were run on Vintage Velvet, Vintage Velvet Creme and Karma Bright White, all from Potlatch. The images are duotones, and the piece was printed with four match colors rather than the four process colors.

"Audible Imagery" Poster
Design: Kenn Tompos
Photography: David Clark Wendt
Copywriting: Leslie Jaffe
Quantity: 500
Budget: $250 out-of-pocket (for paper, type and stats)
Tompos's inspiration for this poster was the photographs themselves. The three images combine to tell a story; the other elements were then added to fill it out. The "Audible Imagery" tagline comes from the various sounds associated with trains.

Credits

pp. 9-11 Werner Design Werks.

pp. 12-13 Designated Designer.

pp. 14-17 Matsumoto Incorporated.

pp. 18-21 Mires Design.

p. 22 Blink.

p. 23 Tom Varisco.

p. 24 Dia Calhoun.

pp. 26-27 Alexander Isley Design.

pp. 28-29 Sommese Design.

pp. 32-33 Barry Power Graphic Design.

pp. 34-36 Abney/Huninghake Design.

p. 37 Nicky Ovitt.

pp. 38-41 Sayles Graphic Design.

pp. 42-43 John DeSantis.

pp. 44-47 Studio MD.

pp. 48-51 Jon Flaming Design.

pp. 52-53 Adams Photography.

pp. 56-57 Graphik On!on.

pp. 58-61 DogStar Design.

pp. 62-65 Art Direction.

pp. 66-67 THARP DID IT.

pp. 68-71 Bielenberg Design.

pp. 74-75 The Design Company.

pp. 76-77 Nancy Doniger Illustration.

pp. 78-81 Mark Oldach Design.

pp. 82-85 Tin Box Studio.

pp. 86-89 Phoenix Creative.

pp. 90-93 Vaughn Wedeen Creative.

pp. 94-96 Winner Koenig.

p. 97 Samata Associates.

p. 101 Artworks.

pp. 102-105 John Evans Design.

pp. 106-109 D. Betz Design.

pp. 110-111 CopperLeaf.

pp. 112-115 Art Chantry.

pp. 188-121 Peterson & Co. .

pp. 122-123 Tom Bonauro.

pp. 124-127 Amy Quinlivan Design.

p. 128 Straight Face Studio.

pp. 10, 11, 15, 16, 19-22, 25, 26, 35, 37, 45-47, 50, 53, 57, 59, 61, 64, 77, 79, 80, 81, 83, 85, 87, 88, 95-97, 101, 105, 110, 111, 114, 120-123, 125-127, studio photography by Pam Monfort.

pp. 16, 17, 49, 113-115, 120, 121, 128, photography by Photo Lab, Inc.

Index